FROM JER

TO

ETERNITY

Call me when you find my name. Art

May God continue you and your family ghout the ups and owns of your life. I love you and hope you enjoy this book. Art

Jerry Maurer

Published by The Farmer and Adele

Copyright © 2012 by Jerry Maurer

ISBN 978-1-105-28189-1

Thank you for purchasing your copy of "From Jer to Eternity."
All profits from sales of this book, beyond printing and shipping
costs, will go to faithalive365.com and the African orphan project
sponsored by the independent church at 463 S. Stagecoach in
Fallbrook, CA, 92028.

WHAT'S INSIDE

Foreword

Years ago my husband and I turned onto a winding country road on the outskirts of Fallbrook, California, following directions to the home where our future daughter-in-law Laura was raised. Jerry and Adele Maurer had invited us to get acquainted over brunch—as we began to meld our lives with theirs into a shared history with our soon-to-be-married kids.

As we turned the last corner onto their lane, we spotted their place: a sentinel wooden farmhouse nestled alone in a few trees at the top of a tall knoll, its many windows opening to hundreds of wild acres with a surrounding panorama of rugged hills soothed and fed by the Santa Margarita River meandering through the valley below. From those windows the Maurers could experience creation's rhythm for land like this: rain and drought, fire and floods, bloom and rest, and the seasonal habits of wildlife that nest and nurture their young in that burly terrain.

So of course it's natural that Jerry and Adele (two of a species of wildlife, of a sort) would raise their wonderful daughter there, in a nest every bit as surprising and nourishing as their surroundings. I hear echoes of her childhood home every time she's with us.

The day we visited, we walked through a wooden arch framing the front walkway, and our eyes promptly turned from the surrounding landscape to the whimsy of the home itself. We had never seen a place like it. Jerry and Adele's creativity and Jerry's woodworking and construction skills had turned their home into an imagination smorgasbord.

A one-story waterfall inside greeted us, and suggested that the pace differed here, quieting whoever walked over the bridge which seemed to float in air. Pictures of family, friends, and life events clustered in nooks told us that relationships matter. A wooden track, installed at ceiling height, supported a train that circled through various rooms. It's meaning? Who knows? But it reminded me to *play!* Surprise after surprise met us as we walked through their home, each requiring some combination of humor, creativity, patience, craftsmanship, and love to complete and to accomplish the intended effect of delighting and enfolding both family and guests.

The stories here hold the same blend of skills, as Jerry has captured his history (his-story) in a series of anecdotes that will bump the hearts, minds, and funny-bones of his readers with eternal truths. His work is refreshing, hilarious, deeply moving, and true. And the applications illustrate a way both to live and to look at our daily lives in Christ--regardless of, and because of, the pain they may hold--with God-glorifying humor, wisdom and joy.

Though the stories build from start to finish, you really can begin anywhere in this book. Just be sure to read them all and consider the questions at the end of each one. You'll be gladder and wiser for it.

--Cheryl Bostrom

Author of *The View from Goose Ridge* and *Children At Promise*

PREFACE

It started with an email to let my friends and relatives know how we were faring in the highly destructive 2007 Rice Canyon wildfire. After a few follow-up notices and a basket full of unsolicited, "When is your next story coming?" I finally admitted to myself that I liked to write. Since each story stands alone the chapters may be read in any order. Although some of those who have read my stories claim the very best chapters are not at the beginning, I suggest you read them in the order presented, as they do build in intensity.

The stories are for anyone who likes to read. The questions at the conclusion of each story, however, are meant for daily devotionals or to stimulate discussions in small groups. The questions are written for Christians or those checking into Christianity.

The stories were sent to all those mentioned in them for verification purposes. There are a few people I was unable to contact. Any differences in memory are either pointed out in the body of the story or in the individual chapter epilogues at the book's conclusion.

If you would like the answers to the questions, send $240,000 to Jerry Maurer, 2267 N. Stagecoach Lane, Fallbrook, CA 92028. (Warning: Do not send cash through the mail.)

In any case, a story a day is all we ask.

Why the title? "Thirty five Days of Purpose" wasn't enough and "The Ghost and Mrs. Maurer" was too obscure.

A handful of chapters were emails meant to inform. The decision was made to leave them "as is" so the sense of urgency, pathos, or impending danger would remain. Such stories have my name at the end.

Jerry Maurer

ACKNOWLEDGEMENTS

Thank you to:

Adele, my wife, the more famous half of The Farmer and Adele.

Laura our daughter (think Little House on the Prairie Laura.)

Barbara Maurer and Cheryl Bostrom who spent untold hours going over my stories and offering great editing advice.

Anna Nimody, who wrote most of the questions numbered "0".

Pastor Phil Sommerville, my nephew, who wrote the lion's share of the questions not numbered "0".

Barbara Pfeiffer, Christine Allen, Judi Buller, Karen Thomas, Kathy Bowman, Rusty Anderson, and Yvonne Weinstein for their time.

The Maurer's Musings group who read my stories and continually encouraged.

The men of Kairos for their enthusiasm.

All the participants in my men's group who have made every Thursday evening special since 1990.

CHAPTER 1   THE FIRE

Wednesday, early am, October 24, 2007   (Re: Oct. 23)

Hello All You Good People,

As you can see, my laptop was one of the things I took with me when Dale McCoy, my great friend and neighbor, and I evacuated. I am writing this because I can't sleep and don't know what else to do. Everyone has a story; here is mine.

We two and a neighbor, Brian Boren, were the only residents who had stayed in our valley. I left the east grove spitters and the roof sprinklers on as we left the house ahead of the impending firestorm. I decided not to leave the east rainbirds on in case water was needed elsewhere. Driving out was surreal; everything was on fire, and just shouldn't have been. Dale and I stopped in our two separate vehicles at the hairpin turn to assess the situation. When we saw the Channel 4 news crew rapidly depart, we decided to continue on, but didn't wish to leave our valley in case officers wouldn't let us back in. We found a great place to wait and look back at the glowing horizon caused by a conflagration beneath. Soon Brian, who had left after us, drove up. It didn't look good at all. Dale asked if Brian had noticed if our house was still there. Brian somberly gave us the bad news: he had stopped to speak with some firemen and they said it probably would not make it. My heart sank. Brian said he was escorted out and barely made it, along with his parrot and two desert turtles.

An hour later, Dale and I decided to go back to see if our homesteads had survived. The embers and smoke grew thicker as we approached, but about three hundred yards before our house would come into sight, our narrow path was blocked by seven pieces of firefighting equipment. No one was going around them.

Back at our safe spot, reality was setting in. The things I didn't get. What would we do? Buy a trailer and rebuild? All the time it would take, but it would not be the same. We tried to sleep a little in the car. Finally, about three and half hours after we left, we decided to try again. What would we see as we rounded the corner onto our street? It was worse than when we left; both sides of the dirt road were ablaze. All that was visible was either on fire or a sea of pocket fires in a sea of black. It was a carpet of orange on black. Had I seen it in a movie, I would have said, "That looks fake." But it wasn't!

I finally saw the big oak tree on the west side of the house and thought, *if that is standing, there is a good chance the house made it.* All I could see was black. Then, unmistakably, the house. And the shop, and the garage and the playhouse. Wow, three hours of thinking it was almost assuredly gone, but it was still there. The Parkers' house to the east? Gone.

Two pumper trucks were there, but they were not needed. The firemen said this place was "dialed in"--with all of the water already on. My own fire hose and one and a quarter inch connection had been ready to go. The firemen had not slept in forty hours, so now was their chance. As I type there are six firemen asleep. Two are on the trampoline, two on the spa's lounge chairs, and two on the lawn. I had offered my three guest bedrooms, but they declined. They sleep while the brush burns around them; the buildings are safe and that is all they care about.

We'll probably have no electricity for several more days. I had installed brass fittings for all above ground plumbing. (Plastic melts, rendering all types of hoses useless.) But the person who had installed the pipe after the meter and before my pressure regulator used plastic, so a gigantic amount of water was seen pouring out down at the bottom of our property. We lost nothing, not one tree. We are a patch of life in a war zone. When the sun comes up it will not be a pleasant sight, but our house here on the hill -- untouched.

Put out some spot fires just north of house, hard work. Tired, just want to shower and go to bed. Oops, no water. Don't want to start generator; might wake firefighters.

Just slept 3 hours, didn't wake up once. Served the guys OJ and cereal for breakfast; they are in here now watching fire news on channel 8. I just asked a firefighter if my house would have made it if no crews had come. He said he saw embers land and extinguish on my wet roof, so no problem. They landed in the trees too, but didn't catch. A lot more to tell, but I am guessing you've heard enough.

A+ in an F zone,

Jerry

DISCUSSION/REFLECTION QUESTIONS

CHAPTER 1   THE FIRE

0. Have you ever lost, or thought you lost, something important to you and then got it back? Recall the story. Contrast the difference in feelings between before and after.

1. If you and your family lost all your material possessions today, to whom would you actually turn to ask to spend the night? To whom would you turn to help you deal with your anguish over the next few weeks and months? Time spent in anguish is time lost. Do you think you would be pretty much over it in twenty years? What could do to get "over it" in weeks, days, or hours?

2. Read 1 Peter 5:7-9 and Ephesians 6:16. Jerry's house was "dialed in." He had done everything he could to be prepared for a forest fire. How prepared are you for a spiritual fire?

3. When a disaster strikes, it's too late to start preparing to protect yourself. We can be engulfed by a spiritual disaster at any moment. What are you doing now to be "dialed in" so that you'll be prepared and protected when attacked?

4. Mentally go through what it would take to get yourself in even better physical shape than you are now. Most of us could profit by doing the same thing spiritually. What could you do to become more "dialed in" spiritually?

CHAPTER 2   WHAT HAPPENED NEXT

Wednesday afternoon October 24, 2007

You probably can imagine how comforted I was to have six firemen and two pumper trucks (one for my neighbor's place, but they stationed themselves here) at my house while smoke and ash filled the air and literally hundreds of small and medium fires burned for 360 degrees around my home. So when the two crews (grateful for so much rest) got orders to assemble down by the mailboxes (a quarter mile away), I was sorry to see them go.

I watched as they joined a red and white convoy winding its way up the canyon. Dale had left minutes earlier in his white dune buggy-ish VW in search of fittings to repair the 12-inch span from the broken water meter to the pressure regulator. Now I was alone.

We live in what some people might call a quiet neighborhood, a really quiet neighborhood. Now it became a different kind of quiet. No sound from diesel engines. No beeping of backing units. No voices hollering instructions. No wind. No sound from squawk boxes. The many smoke plumes added to the eeriness of the scene. The multitude of fires were surely making noise, but their combined sounds did not reach the deck where I surveyed what had happened in the preceding hours. There are not too many people living in this part of the valley, but right then I was the *only* one! Usually one can hear the Santa Margarita River, which flows westward just a few yards to the north. But there was absolutely no sound. No birds, no dogs, no anything. My own sigh broke the silence. A shift in my weight caused a wooden plank to creak. Fallbrook was evacuated. Here I was standing just outside the kitchen, feeling sorry for the Parkers while for myself, blessed. What is fair about that? I knew I was not the last living thing on earth, it just felt like it.

In the past whenever I saw a fire, I would be on it in seconds. Now I stood there silently and alone, watching fires of varying dimensions in, truthfully, every single direction. You have heard someone say, "Unreal!" before. Well, at that moment I was in the heart of unreality.

Then it happened. A small fire that had been slowly growing just on the other side of the river caused a twenty-foot tree to erupt into flames. This set off some dry brush just on the other side of what used to be the train tracks that ran from Temecula to the ocean. Soon a 60-foot hill became a mountain of fire. I looked at the blaze. Then I looked at the distance from it to a dry, two-acre section of unburned brush, which fantastically had made it through the night. Simultaneously, I felt the developing breeze on my unshaven face even as I knew a call to 911 to report an uninhabited hill on fire to a dispatcher (who knew several hundred square miles of California were on fire) would be absurd.

I remembered that I had 125 feet of one-and-a-quarter inch fire hose, scads of garden hose, hose bibs running all the way down my hill...and how I currently had zero water pressure. I considered ripping off my shirt and swatting at flames as I had once seen in a bad movie. (True, it didn't work there, but you couldn't just have the character stand and watch, could you?) No, no sir, I needed water.

Ever seen an episode of MacGyver? Think of him when you picture this: I went to the fridge, and there in the back was a can of soda (7-Up, green). I cut off the ends, split it lengthwise, got some hose clamps, a couple pieces of inner tube, and tools from the shop, and headed down the fifty yards to where the FPUD's plastic field box had melted onto a short, but critical piece of plastic schedule-eighty pipe. The hole in the partially melted, mottled, warped, blackened pipe was about the size of a fifty-cent piece. I placed a folded piece of inner tube over the hole and then wrapped the can around the assembly and started to fashion worm-screw hose clamps long enough to fit around my Jerry-rigged patch. Did you know there are different width hose clamps? Did you know a narrow width clamp fits and works perfectly when placed into a wider width clamp? Did you know, however, that when that wider width end is placed into the narrower receiving end to complete the encirclement of the project, it is what experts call a "no go"? Well, I know that ... now. Time wasted. Did you know that plumbing is usually not a stress-filled job? Did you know that when you are working on a plumbing job on which the survival of your home may depend, tension begins to become a factor? Can you imagine looking over your shoulder a handful of times and seeing that the fire is much more advanced than the last time you checked? (As in that classic Twilight Zone starring Earl Holliman, "Where is everybody?") But then, you are truly never alone.

Lord, help me stay calm so I can do this. I was able to make three bands of two different widths to secure the can to the pipe. I needed a fourth because the breach was before the regulator. Where could I get another? I quickly took one off a vehicle up top. With the fire raging, I strapped on the fourth and turned the city water brass ball valve on. Water poured out as if I were Buster Keaton and not John Wayne. Oh no! This couldn't be happening! I had done such a good job. I planned. I executed. I failed! Going to lose the house after all that?

Then I heard a roar. A helicopter flew over me, then scooped up 500 gallons of water from a reservoir one of my neighbors had made a few years earlier. The 'copter dashed low over my house and dropped a load of algae-filled water onto the fire. On his way back, another joined him, and then another. Incredibly a fourth 'copter, this one capable of sucking up 2,000 gallons in just a few seconds, joined the other three. For just short of an hour they made continuous loops from 250 yards SE of our house to the reservoir, just over my house 140 yards to the fire and back. Talk about a bucket brigade!

I guess if you are MacGyver and get saved by Wonder Woman you don't complain. I guess if you are Jerry and get saved at all, and did nothing to deserve it, you don't complain. Near the end of all this, my good friends Brad and Tom pulled up in Tom's F150 and recorded the process with their respective video and still cameras. Dale was successful in his quest and replaced the section of pipe.

When Dale showed me the broken piece, we saw that my patch had held, but the water pressure had caused a second hole on the bottom of the pipe. I didn't feel quite so bad.

I was so thankful to still have a window to look through—even at the temporarily burnt earth crust. I knew that God would fix the view.

Jerry

DISCUSSION/REFLECTION QUESTIONS

CHAPTER 2   WHAT HAPPENED NEXT

0. Can you think of a time you were nervous about an action you should probably take? Not a competition or dreaded activity, but something that would probably have a dire consequence if you failed. Consider sharing how you handled it.

1. Is it possible that God would purposely put you in a situation you can't get out of despite your best efforts? Explain. Now, read Judges 7. What was God's reason for thinning out Gideon's troops? If you were to have experienced this event for yourself, what would it have done for your faith?

2. Read Isaiah 31:1, Psalm 20:7, and Zechariah 4:6. What "horses and chariots" might you be tempted to trust—instead of God--to solve your problems?

3. Read 2 Kings 6:1-17. Elisha's servant was given a glimpse of reality beyond what he could see with his eyes. If you could use your "eyes of faith" and trust in God's reality as Elisha did, what impact would that have on your life and on the way you react to things? What prevents you from having that kind of trust?

4. Read Psalm 121 then turn this Psalm into a prayer. What can you celebrate from this passage? Thank God for those things. Are you convicted about an attitude, thought or action that does not honor God after reading this passage? Confess that to God. Do you feel called to take some kind of action after reading this Psalm? If so commit yourself before God to take action and ask for God's strength. Do you know someone who needs to put his or her trust in the hope and promise of this Psalm? Pray for that person now.

CHAPTER 3   I THOUGHT

Officials are still not letting people into our part of Fallbrook. I also found out there will be no electricity for more than a week (until Nov 8). I may not go to church Sunday, as I might not be allowed back in. Only two neighbors got in somehow; the rest are all out, somewhere. No mail, no trash pick-up on Monday. The empty cans of my neighbors from last Monday are all still sitting out, adding to the otherworldly feel of this drama.

I heard from Dale and Brian that is was okay to go to town but that nothing was open. Dale said there was burned-out stuff to see...well, burned out stuff was all around me. It has been sixty hours since we evacuated to a different part of this valley. I figured I would check on the homes of some friends. Just as I was preparing to go out to my car, about 250 yards to the east I saw a formerly fortunate tree go from a small fire to one completely involved, joining the fate of most of its neighbors.

How fragile life? So many things this experience has taught. I had thought in that first morning when the sun rose everything would be black. Everything was white, the gray fallen ash appearing as old snow. I thought no more big blazes would be starting in this area for quite a while, but I was wrong. I thought the owl that patrolled our portion of the world for field mice, gophers, and rabbits would come back to its lucky tree, but she didn't. I thought I would get a few replies from the friends and family to whom I sent my email, but instead I got blessings from them, and offers, and returned human emotion through the internet and requests to send it on, and notes saying it had been sent on, and emails from people to whom I hadn't sent it, and from people I had never met, and prayers. I thought all of my huge preparatory water use and subsequent 200-psi leak would cause a large water bill, but the meter is toast! I thought I would be different inside, but it is still *me*.

Got in the car and went to town--it was as foretold. There were almost no other people besides the many firefighting convoys, police cars, parked military personnel, and some service trucks. All shops closed. Streets empty.

(Note: About 18 years ago I decided to get the very best ground cover for fire; do you know what the very best ground cover for fire is? I researched and found that it is <u>dirt</u>. Dead stuff burns, live stuff burns, dirt does not burn. Got dirt? That is why I weed whack so much.)

After my little trip to town, I went past my driveway to check on my neighbors' homes. On the way back I stopped, got out and took a picture with my cell phone of our home from the east. The black and ash stops suddenly at the dirt. . .dirt doesn't burn. I sent the picture to my wife's and daughter's cell phones. My daughter text-messaged back from Arizona, "You are such a good weed whacker. I actually miss waking up to it." I don't know why, but somehow that makes me nostalgic for when she was so little I could just pick her up and swing her. I can still hear her laugh. A few minutes later a second message read, "I want to come home so bad, I guess it will just have to wait 'til Christmas." Must be some father-daughter thing that gets me right here.

A little later some firemen were out checking hot spots and took a short break to eat lunch out by the playhouse and its little pond. I let them know they were welcome to move to the side yard where there was even more shade if they wished. I told them about the trampoline and that it was good for a nap. I offered them ice and drinks, but they said they were fine. As I left I heard one of them say, "What are a bunch of firemen going to do with a trampoline?" The others laughed; I pretended I didn't hear.

Dale and I made chili from a can and ham steak on the barbecue and then watched a movie on DVD. Seemed strange sitting in a remote darkened valley with all that was going on and watching a movie. During the movie there was a knock at the door. Dale told me later he had thought it might be looters. It was the firemen from earlier wanting to know if it was okay to sleep the night on the trampoline. I offered my guest bedrooms, but they said they would just rather sleep outside. All but the jokester that is; he slept in the truck.

Jerry

DISCUSSION/REFLECTION QUESTIONS

CHAPTER 3   I THOUGHT

0. Recall something you just knew was true, but then discovered you were wrong. Do you admit your error easily? Or is it harder for you than for most?

1. Under what circumstances do you feel the most homesick?

2. Read 2 Corinthians 5:1-10. For what is Paul homesick? How does he describe the symptoms of his homesickness? Have you ever felt the way Paul describes? When?

3. Paul has never seen heaven or been there, so how can he be homesick for it? Is heaven more real to Paul than his current life on earth? Explain.

4. How will your awareness of the reality of heaven influence the way you live your life on earth? Are you living like heaven is a reality?

CHAPTER 4   MENTAL EXERCISE

Sunday October 28, 2007

We thank you for your prayers, encouragement and many generous offers for help and lodging. The number of emails on the fires and their heartfelt contents is completely uplifting. When a friend told me my first email was in the paper, I thought Brian might get in trouble because the story mentioned he had two desert turtles (an endangered species). When I told him this, he laughed and said it was all right, because that was the least of his worries, and anyway, he had documents proving he could have them.

The evacuation order for all of Fallbrook was lifted on Saturday. Shortly thereafter our valley started coming back to life. It was fantastic to see everyone at church. I went to both services, to worship and hear more stories. After that I picked up Adele in San Diego; she knew what to expect from descriptions, pictures I'd sent and the news. She will be glad to get our electricity back. (That will total about 20 days with no electricity.)

During the few hours I thought the house was probably destroyed and while waiting in the car trying to get a little sleep, I took a mental trip through the entire house. I saw the things I thought no one would ever not see again. Everything fell into one of two categories. The purchased things meant absolutely nothing, while things we had made were paramount. You know, the tangible things that helped transform our house to a home. I had brought out the wooden alphabet puzzle I made for Laura for her third birthday. A photographic history of time with her lay behind each of the twenty-six pieces. I was sorry that I had not also brought the large framed map of the United States Laura and I had made for her mother using old stamps we had collected from each of those states.

As for the intangibles, what could vanquish them?

On the way out on my imaginary tour, right by the front door where we keep letters to be mailed in an old spring type holder sat our annual termite insurance payment.

Dale read the first email a few days ago. He said, "Yes, that is just how it was, but I can't believe you didn't mention the burning oak." Here's the story: While driving successfully from our safe spot to the house, on the right was an oak tree hollowed by fire, burning and glowing from the inside. Dale wanted to stop and take a picture, but knew that was no time for cameras.

Not far from there is a route Adele and I take for a daily walk. It is one of my favorites. The shady trail winds through old oak, spruce, and pepper trees along the Santa Margarita River and, via stepping-stones, crosses Rainbow Creek. Don't know if this fire was man or nature-made, but it affected both. This particular trail is still there (remember, dirt doesn't burn.) The brush along the trail is gone, but I think many of the trees, although greatly damaged, will make it. I saw a large drooping cactus like a many-eared, sorrowful hound. I saw a huge, determined stinkbug covered in ash. I took a picture with my cell phone (I should have set my keys next to him so you could see his size). His body was dented, not cracked--reminiscent of a trunk lid on a '57 Buick struck by a bowling ball dropped from the fourth story. He was headed somewhere; he meant business.

The day after I saw the melancholy cactus and the quiet, wounded stinkbug, true cacophony erupted. As if to collectively mourn the fire's destruction, three or four huge flocks of crows covered the trees in a small canyon about sixty yards away. In the remnant of that spruce grove, hundreds of crows perched and cawed relentlessly...none flying, each cawing. Incredible! (Alfred Hitchcock came to mind.)

In church, the pastor asked some of those listening to share the first thing they grabbed as they evacuated. From the side of the fridge I had grabbed an old handwritten list entitled, "Evacuation, in case of." While driving to bring Adele home I was thinking: knowing what I know now, what would I have done differently? I determined there was one thing: I would not have weed-whacked those first 18 years, just this year when it was actually needed.

Jerry

DISCUSSION/REFLECTION QUESTIONS

CHAPTER 4   MENTAL EXERCISE

0. If you only had time to save three items from your house, what would you save (assuming your family is safe and the size of the items do not matter)? What makes those particular items valuable to you?

1. Intangible things are fireproof. What intangible thing do you treasure the most?

2. Read Luke 12:13-34. Summarize what Jesus is teaching in one or two sentences.

3. According to this passage, what is truly valuable and what is not? What will identify a person as a follower of Christ?

4. What does your current lifestyle say about the things you value? Are there some things you should prioritize differently?

CHAPTER 5   LOOTERS

Wednesday, October 31, 2007

A few days ago Loren Martin (from my Thursday night men's group) dropped by and we caught up on what we knew. He told me about our common friends, the Goodmans, who were out of state when the fires hit. Their boat and some other equipment burned just behind their home. Their house was about to go up in flames, but a pumper truck arrived in time to save it. Two days later, a neighbor of the Goodmans was patrolling the area in his car when he saw a skinhead on a three-wheeled ATC where he shouldn't be. The little hoodlum was going around asking people if they needed help cleaning up in exchange for money. Usually people said they did not, but if no one was home, the tank-top-wearing coward would call his buddy in a nearby truck and they would rob the place. The neighbor chased the would-be thief directly into a police blockade. The police used the skinhead's cell phone to call the accomplice. They caught him too, and recovered stolen property from several different homes.

On Wednesday, October 31, 2007 (Halloween), Adele went to town to shop and dry the clothes. (Still no electricity--our dryer is 220 volts and we don't have the correct connection to our generator. I'll have to get one.) One good thing about the electricity being off, we won't have to set all of our clocks back this weekend.

With the fire danger over, I prepared to wash the fire-retardant gel off the east side of our home. It looked like soap and came off easily. While I was at it, I thought I might as well rinse off the entire house. As I came around after I had finished the back, I saw a strange car stopped at the top of our driveway. Three people were hunkered down very low in their seats. I could only see the tops of their heads; the driver wore a headband. I figured they probably saw the garage with no empty stalls and thought they would look elsewhere for a house with no one home. They then drove slowly down our private driveway. Plenty of lookie-loos had wandered the area in the past few days, but none of them were bold enough to come up here. I turned off the hose bib and went to my deck to see which way they would go. Left was the only way out of this valley and right was to my neighbors. They turned right. I watched as they went up the private driveway for the Duffers and what had been the Parker house. It looked as if Duffer was not home. Dale was working in town, so as I went to my car, I called Brian to let him know I was following the strangers. He was in Escondido, and asked to be kept informed. As I drove up that driveway I could see no one was at the Duffers. When I crested the top at the Parkers' I could see the car was now empty. I must admit, things did not seem right, especially with three to one odds. I was a little relieved when I saw that one of the three was a woman, and then I noticed that the other two were in their eighties. They were serving with the Red Cross from various states back east. I had two conversations at once: one of the men wanted to talk all about the fire and the woman wanted to know about my home and what it was like living all the way out here. She wanted to know how many hours it took to get to a grocery store. When I told her fourteen minutes, she seemed disappointed.

Upon Adele's return I told of the "looters" and then, knowing that we have had a grand total of one carload of trick-or-treaters, and that was back before the turn of the century, I looked for the just-in-case bags of candy. Butterfingers.

I went to town to buy another five-gallon container and filled it and our other two five-gallon cans with gas. No electricity expected for several more days. I also purchased more lantern oil and a replacement bulb for a flashlight. Ready for the long haul.

Adele wanted to get out of the house, so we went to see that rat-who-cooks movie. When we got home, we noticed our electricity supply had returned. A couple hours of October left and it was "on." Phone service was another story, so we used our cells. (If you don't have our cell numbers, just call and I will give them to you.)

Greg Coppock brought his TV crew out here yesterday. (His sound man is the lead male vocalist in our praise band, and the cameraman is the former head of adult ministries at our church.

When the filming was over he said that he would give the footage to his editor, who turned out to be the husband of our good friend Janet. Small world!) The half-hour episode of Total Victory will firstl air Wednesday Nov. 7, 2007 at 8 pm on cable Ch. 19.

Oh, there are a couple of things I must tell you. Firstly, the firemen said the A-frame burned down, but when I looked out in the morning, it was still there. Maybe they meant some other house somewhere. Secondly, before her evacuation, our neighbor Carla came over; her baby was supposed to arrive early next week, but the car wouldn't start and the bridge was out, so I had to deliver her baby. No electricity, no water, no anesthesia, Caesarean! With the smoke and embers swirling, the baby turned out to be twins! She named the first one Jerrold and the second Gerri-Anne. Well ladies and gentlemen, this second thing isn't quite what happened, but it is just about the only ingredient missing, isn't it?

Jerry

DISCUSSION/REFLECTION QUESTIONS

CHAPTER 5   LOOTERS

0. Have you ever been robbed or looted? Have ever gone into a situation that looked bad and then turned out to be completely different that what you had been thinking? Recall how you felt.

1. How do you feel about criminals who try to profit from other people's tragedies? How did you feel when the miscreant in Jerry's story was caught?

2. Read John 10:10. How is the devil described and contrasted with Jesus? If this is true, why do so many people struggle to fully obey Jesus?

3. Read John 10:1-5. How do we protect ourselves from those who would rob us of experiencing life to the full? How are sheep able to protect themselves? Can they protect themselves? What does that suggest about what we must do to protect ourselves? What's the consequence if we don't?

4. Do you get as upset about what the devil is doing to your friends and neighbors as you do about a looter looting a house? Why or why not? What can you do in response?

CHAPTER 6   PASS...ON THIS CHAPTER

A list of OPPOSITES, by J. R. Maurer

Blu-ray	Blurry
Bar food	Barf food
Osama	Aunt Bee
Gamblers Anonymous	NYSE
Compromise	Common sense
Something	
Fell into skeptic's trap door	Fell into septic's trap door
Education	Prime time TV
Kindle	Ken doll
Fans of Jiminy Cricket	Fans of Yemeni cricket
Nooks and crannies	Crooks and nannies
He's a prince of a man	Here' prints of that man
China Syndrome	Science
A Toyota	A toy Yoda
1,000 apples	1,000 AAPLs
Halle Berry	Halliburton
Dr. Spock	Mr. Spock
Leonard Nimoy	Leonard McCoy
Penn State	State Pen
Toilet water	Toilet water
Del Taco	Delta Co.
Taco Bell's burrito	Pachelbel's Bolero
Apostle's Creed	Apollo Creed
Hard breaking putt	Heart breaking putt
TP	Teepee
One bad Tic Tac	One bad tactic
Bigoted	Bighearted

He robbed the profit	He robed the prophet
Generally	General Lee
Pass...on this chapter	Pass on this chapter
Wife problems	Wifi problems
The truth is in the details	Based on a true story
Guilt	Forgiveness
Frees butterflies	Freeze butterflies
People	Peep hole
Girl of my dreams	Grill of my dreams
Hedwig	Hagrid
Cry me a river	Crimean River
Sold out	Soul doubt
Sarah Palin	Sarah, Plain and Tall
Nowhere	Now here
Sandwiches on the beach	Sand which is on the beach
One man, one vote	Same day registration
Madonna	The Madonna
Cindy Sheehan	Cindy Sheehan's son
Sincere	Sin seer
Being accepted	Being excepted
Casaba	Kielbasa
War	Tyranny
Financers	Find answers
Unique silverish necklace	Unique silverfish necklace
He's a real high roller	He's a real eye roller
Mr. Opportunity	Missed her opportunity
One Rainbow Slushie please	One Rainbow Sushi please
A Broadway star tried Rigatoni	A star tried to rig a Tony
Bareness and Blight	Baroness Ann Blythe
The etymology bugged him	Entomology bugged him
It was a long silly bus	It was a long syllabus

Marionberry	Marry and bury
Pulitzer Prize	Pullet surprise
Messy anecdote	Messianic dote
On or off the field	Honor off the field

DISCUSSION/REFLECTION QUESTIONS

CHAPTER 6   PASS...ON THIS CHAPTER

0. Jerry hoped his list would spark some laughter. Can you remember a time you purposefully made several people laugh out loud?

1. Have you ever wished that something in your life were opposite the way it really is? Maybe you would like to change something going on around you, something you're involved in, something about your personality, something about your spouse (oops, if you're smart you won't say that one out loud), or something about another relationship. What in your life do you wish were opposite?

2. Read Ephesians 4:20-32. This passage offers a whole list of opposites. Identify as many as you can and actually place them into two columns. What heading would you give each column?

3. What does Ephesians 4:24 say God created us to be like? How do you react to this? What does it mean that we are created to be like that? If God intends us to be like that, but we're not, what are we missing?

4. Your list gives you a vision for what God would like to accomplish in your life and a way to evaluate your growth. What needs improvement? How will you cooperate with the work God wants to do in you to grow in this area? Be specific.

CHAPTER 7 A CRUISE

Dec. 14, 2007 (RE: June 1959)

Saturday Adele and I left Fallbrook for our first cruise. Immediately upon stepping aboard, a certain semi-pleasant smell (probably from the galley) that my olfactory had not encountered in half a century brought back vivid memories from almost five decades earlier.

I was nine and on one of the exceedingly few vacations ever taken by my parents. My father was a dairyman (milk cows in the morning, process milk during the day, milk the cows at night.) No weekends off. No time off. No holidays off. No days off. Work 365.2524 days a year. Then, suddenly, my father, mother, twelve-year-old sister Dixie and I were sailing toward a summer-long stay in Holland. My first time on a vacation and I found myself on a passenger liner on my way to see my father's side of the family.

The first morning at sea was sunny. My mother, sister, and I went to visit the purser. I left them for a few seconds to walk around the elevator shaft. This separated me from the rest of the family as the "down" stairs on one side were many more than the "up" stairs on the other (the fact that the floor changed color each time I went around should have raised a red flag -- *should* have.) I finally found my self at the entrance to the theater on the lowest deck. Running back to the purser's deck showed that I was now on my own. I went back to the theater, where no ticket taker met me. I cautiously opened the door; still no ticket taker. I sat down and watched the last forty-five minutes of Gigi. Not a great action picture when you are nine. When it ended, I had no idea where to go, so I followed about ten, maybe eleven kids (who turned out to be all brothers and sisters). They soon went into their cabin. By a big stroke of luck, I recognized our cabin number about twenty yards away, just around the corner. Went in, everyone was happy, but none more than I.

During the night we hit what my mom called the tail end of a hurricane. Dixie and I spent the entire next day in our stateroom, seasick, but not my dad. He had sea legs; at least that is what he called them. I wanted sea legs. To be able to walk where ever you wished and not worry about the roll (the left, port, going up and down), or the pitch (bow going up and down), or the yaw (aft swishing left and right.)

The next day, although still in a state of advanced queasiness, I was determined to walk the halls with my father. (We were not allowed on the outside decks because the day before a man had fallen from one deck to another and died.) You sort of walk slowly uphill and then quickly down while simultaneously walking splayed to the left followed by splayed to the right. Maybe just getting out of the cabin or concentrating on walking instead of what may or may have been in my stomach made the difference, but taking action most assuredly made me feel at least 68% better.

The following day a few more people ventured out in the hallways even though we were probably in the worst throes of the hurricane. So there I was, feeling pretty good on my ever-improving sea legs, going for a walk with my dad. Even the mid-day storm gloom did not stop me from whistling while on our stroll. (Before I go any further, I must ask you a question: Did you whistle when you were little? Well, I did, all the time. People don't seem to whistle anymore. When was the last time you heard someone whistle a tune? Way back in the middle of the last century, when you heard someone whistling you knew they were happy, and that, somehow, made you happy, too. If you could whistle, you could have your music wherever you went, and the batteries would never run out.)

I mean, what else was there to do besides watch Gigi again, play Bingo, eat, or get rid of what you had eaten... one way or the other? (I much preferred one way!) As the big ship violently pitched and rolled, people hung on the rails like osteoporosis patients on ice skates for the first time. My father and I could walk right down the middle of the hall. A nun asked my dad if she could have a word with him. When my dad later told the story to my mom, I heard the details of their conversation: The nun was praying that this ship would make it through the hurricane safely and she did not think it appropriate that he (my dad) let his son (me) whistle (I'm guessing a happy tune) while we were all in such a terrible situation, being out in the Atlantic in a hurricane and all. I guess he told her he thought whistling was okay, because he never asked me to desist.

Jerry

From somewhere off the coast of Mexico

DISCUSSION/REFLECTION QUESTIONS

CHAPTER 7   A CRUISE

0. When you were a youngster did you usually feel safe when your parents were around? When do you feel safe now?

1. Read Eph 4:11-16. Paul is speaking to Christians in these verses. What might he be referring to in verse 14? Give some concrete examples. How have you experienced this yourself?

2. According to verses 11-13, what will give us our "sea legs" so that we can avoid the situation described in verse 14?

3. According to verses 15-16, what will be the evidence that we have spiritual "sea legs"? What will that look like in your group or church?

4. On a scale of 1-10, rate yourself (not others) on how well you are doing compared to the description given in verses 15-16. 1 = failing miserably, 10 = doing fantastically. Based on what you are being taught in Ephesians 4:11-16, what specific actions do you need to take to improve?

CHAPTER 8   A CHRISTMAS STORY

December 23, 2007

Whenever our small family was about to leave a place after a great vacation, I would do a final room check for belongings. Then as we were just about to exit, Adele would say, "Goodbye room," or "Goodbye villa," or "Goodbye (wherever we were)" and then do a pretend sniff as if she were about to cry. She would do this because we'd had a good time and even if we did come back, we would probably not get that same unit. We might never see it again. That small ritual reminds me why I love her so.

I don't know when it started, but when I squeeze her or our daughter, Laura, three times, it is secret code for "I--love--you." One may squeeze at just about any time. These two traditions, plus the fact that Laura and her loving husband, Andrew, are here to celebrate the birth of our Savior, have given me pause to reminisce. Actually, the reminiscing began when Laura said she hadn't been home since their wedding eight months earlier.

I remember when Laura was forty seconds old, breathing comfortably and not crying. For the first time in her life she could stretch without limit, which, as her uncle Ralph had said, would be a little frightening to her. So with the little finger and thumb of my left hand I returned her out-spread fists closer to her body to stop her slight cry of anguish as I captured this amazing moment with the camera in my right hand.

I remember when she was just a few days old and, during one of the rare times in her life she was not sleeping well, I picked her up out of the bassinette, lay back down in bed and placed her entire body curled up on the top half of my chest. She moved her ear right over my heart and quickly fell asleep. I think I've loved her since before she was born, but that night she stole my heart forever.

I remember when she was eight months old and we flew up to Hughes Stadium in Sacramento to watch some of my athletes compete in the High School California State Track Meet. I remember how she laughed when the crowd roared.

I remember several months later when Adele was not due back from a horse show for another day. I let Laura talk to her mother on the phone. Laura said, "Hi." Later she said, "Bye." And then it happened as I hung up. Laura was standing in the middle of the kitchen, tears instantaneously welling in her eyes, her right hand ceremoniously reaching out to the phone high on the wall as she said her first sentence, "Bye, bye, Mommy!" She didn't quite understand phones back then. She probably mistakenly thought she would never see her mother again. Rip my heart out, throw it on the ground and stomp on it. "Bye, bye, Mommy." Oh, I swooped her up, spun her around and around, held her tight, and tried to make her understand that Mommy would be home after just one more night-night.

I remember when we were all outside at Grandma and Grandpa's and from a hand full of yards away she gave me the let's-play-chase-right-now-Daddy-look. I smiled, but before I could say, "no" she turned away from me and began the all-out sprint of a three year old toward the busy street less than ten yards away. I didn't think I would catch her in time; my shouting was no deterrent to her efforts at speed. I dove at the last possible half second and grabbed one of her ankles. Laura came down hard; her face hit the road's packed earthen shoulder--safe by four feet! No one knew if she was crying because some part or her hurt or because she thought I had made her hit the ground on purpose. It was probably some of each. How our lives could have changed in those two seconds. What does a father do in such a situation? Hold her, hug her, and tell a sobbing Laura that her father loves her with all that he is. It's hard to have your heart in your throat when someone else has your heart.

I remember seeing her small body two years later lying motionless at the bottom of our long driveway after she had fallen off her bike. I remember driving a little too fast to the town hospital. I remember how it felt to finally hear her cry. It's hard to have your heart in your throat when someone else has your heart... hard, but not impossible.

I remember teaching her a little about track and field, using "string hurdles" in the side yard. I remember her announcing that she would like to be baptized. I remember her first day of high school. I remember getting to the track meets just in time to see her run the high hurdles, then the triple jump, then the low hurdles, then the mile relay. I remember the literally hundreds of soccer, lacrosse, and field hockey games. I remember when we flew up to the same Hughes Stadium in Sacramento to watch *Laura* compete in the High School California State Track Meet. I remember saying goodbye to her at the airport as she went off to college.

I remember the day she graduated from the University. I remember her first day on the job as a dental hygienist. I remember the day before her long awaited outdoor wedding as we practiced on the covered deck looking at a downpour in a record drought year. I remember her saying, "Daddy, I really want to ride out in the carriage with you." I remember the absolute clarity of the next day, especially as we rode around the lake together. I remember her taking my right arm as I escorted her down the aisle. I remember reaching over and squeezing her left hand three times as we walked toward the young man who would soon be her husband. I remember dancing with her to "I Loved Her First" as they showed family pictures in the background of her growing up.

I remember one week later, just after their honeymoon, while Andrew was outside putting the final touches on the loaded rental truck, as they were about to drive off to Arizona to start their married life together. She stood at the base of the bridge by the front door and said a few words that pierced my soul-- something no spear could. She was facing the front door but within earshot of me (a little past the other end of the bridge) when she said, "Bye-bye house." Rip my heart out ...

Now that I have written this, it is much more of an Easter story isn't it? The two stories each have the best (happiest of) endings though, don't they?

Well, Laura, and Andrew can stretch without limit, and no one can stop them, let alone with the little finger and thumb of their left hand.

DISCUSSION/REFLECTION QUESTIONS

CHAPTER 8   A CHRISTMAS STORY

0. Think of a time you knew something was going to happen, and it did, even though you did not want it to. How did you handle it?

1. Why would Jerry let his daughter go? Why would God let us go?

2. Read 1 John 3:1. Jerry shared fond memories of moments with his daughter. What fond memories might God have of His relationship with you? How do Jerry's memories help you better understand God's love for us? Do you find it easy or hard to imagine that God loves you in the same way Jerry loves his daughter?

3. Read Deuteronomy 31:8 and Luke 15:11-32. What do you hear God saying to you right now through these verses?

4. Say a prayer that expresses how you are feeling towards God right now.

CHAPTER 9 POOP HAPPENS

(RE: late October 2007)

Immediately after the Fallbrook fire of ought-seven, several
people felt sorry for me. How awful it must be! Wife outside the
evacuation zone, no electricity, no phones, everything burned
around the house, no water, our valley devoid of people, ashes
everywhere, smoke damage, messes to clean up, and if I left the
area I would not be allowed back in. I tried to tell them
otherwise, but for over a month people were just certain I must
have been in terrible straits.

Well, let me address these points. Adele was safe at a horse show
in Albuquerque and probably had it far better than most
evacuees. As for no electricity, I had a 4,000-watt gas powered
generator and several large, filled gas cans (plus full car tanks
which could be siphoned, if needed). Furthermore, the steaks,
ham steaks, hot dogs, roasts and much more could be cooked on
the barbeque (had an extra propane tank for that, too). I also
had plenty in the pantry. The phone lines and poles were down,
but I could charge my cell phone and take advantage of the
excellent reception out here.

Yes, everything was burned around us, but not much on our
land. Several big trees got scorched and hopefully will survive.
(We learned they were ours when the fire exposed the old metal
posts pointing out surveyor monuments.) The failed Barricade
foam rinsed off easily. Then the windows needed washing, but
nothing out of the ordinary.

Sure, the view had changed, but we were all safe. It was like
catching the winning pass in the super bowl, and then getting to
your car and noticing one tire was a little low. True, we lacked
water pressure, but my good friend and neighbor, Dale, handily
repaired that now semi-infamous one-foot section of plastic pipe.
(And in a pinch, I could tap any of the several gallons of bottled
water, a spa, some ponds, plus a river running freely several
yards down the hill.) Again, few people remained in our valley,
but Dale and I had lots of great food to cook, books, DVD's, big
TV with satellite connection, along with computers and Wi-Fi.
No ashes coated our house or blew in the wind. Amazingly, the

heavy smoke had caused no smoke damage inside or out. I suppose most of it went up and away. As far as messes to clean up, I had to dry out my fire hoses and hang them from the big oak. Had to put 'em back, so I put 'em back. That was it.

Dale and I were eating and living like kings: Dale's plant had closed, (no one allowed in town) and I had recently retired. I was on call for jury duty for a month, but never got called in, partly because the courts closed for a week due to the fires. Living like a king is pretty nice. "It's good to be the king." But after a while you gotta do something! So I decided to repaint the arched gate out front. In one day it went from a nice white to a really nice white. Boy did it look clean! You should have seen it.

The next morning on my way out I noticed little black hand prints up the outside of my freshly painted gate and down the inside. It just couldn't be a diminutive, crazed, mythical mechanic; I figured that a raccoon that had recently walked through ash had traipsed up then down the gate. (After some spraying and wiping, the paint looked almost as good as new-- almost.) Later I got the feeling there were fewer goldfish in the front pond than previously. Don't raccoons relish fish?

The evacuation order was lifted the day Adele was to return. She said she saw some fresh coyote poop on the roof of the walk-in closet Dale and I had built for her. (Looking back it was probably a mistake to build that closet; since a small closet = a small wardrobe and a huge closet = a huge wardrobe. Yes, a mistake.) We have a deck that wraps around a large portion of our house and it is a small step to the closet's roof. Well, my nickname isn't The Farmer for nothing. I know coyote poop when I see it, and this was no coyote poop. It was raccoon poop! Probably containing goldfish bones. (I don't like this raccoon. Have you ever thrown recycled goldfish off a roof using a shovel? Well I have. Big step down from king!)

The next morning I spotted fresh raccoon prints on the deck and not only more raccoon poop on the roof, but raccoon pee too, right there on *my* roof. This was personal now. Then more bad news: all the goldfish had disappeared from the pond, including the fancy one with the big bug eyes that Adele liked so much. Liked.

This is where my extensive education comes into play. I remember reading somewhere that many animals mark their territory with urine, and that sometimes ranchers have urinated around the perimeter to ward off wolves. So I thought about those wolves. Well, two can pee that game. That's right, I went right out there on the roof and set a large snap-type mouse trap right on his favorite dumping ground, adjacent to the wall about one foot from the window's edge. It wouldn't kill him, but it would, well, you know, scare the poop out him.

The next morning I checked the trap -- not sprung, but no used raccoon food either. I wondered if he had seen the trap and figured he wasn't dealing with your average man. Then I saw his handiwork. He had knocked one of the attached planter boxes I had made off the outer edge of the deck's railing to the ground, one story below.

The following morning the trap had not moved and I found no evidence of the raccoon on the roof. However, such was not the case when I went out to the detached deck about twenty-five yards west of our home. Two different sets of raccoon prints trailed across the fairly new replacement spa cover. They had walked through the dew of the grass and the moisture from their paws mixed with the dust on the cover, to paint a mud fresco of their antics. Their antics included a frolic on the cover, followed by a ripping of its simulated leather hide and a gnawing of the white Styrofoam beneath. I don't like these raccoons.

I then went to the flag gate to check my handiwork from the day before. There they were, two sets of opposable-thumb prints set in my cement. Intolerable! The nerve of those guys... a permanent reminder of the two print-leaving, goldfish-eating, poop-pooping, planter-crashing, spa cover-ripping, cement-vandalizing varmints. Varmints, I say! So I got Adele and showed her the latest escapades of my demon tormentors from hell. (I can say hell, can't I? Yes, demon tormentors from hell.) Everything was going great until she saw the couple's prints in the new cement. That is when it happened. She named them. She actually named them! Once they are named you're sunk. (As my Washington nephews would say in their best Eeyore voice, "We're doomed.") Now that they have names I can't even throw rocks at them! Oh, the humanity! (I can hear my mother's voice now, "Jerrold Ray, you stop that this instant!")

I give up; I am no match for my wife, Elly May Clampett, and Robby and Roberta Raccoon.

DISCUSSION/REFLECTION QUESTIONS
CHAPTER 9   POOP HAPPENS

0. What did your mother call you when she was mad at you? (Have you ever noticed that when you are angry at someone you often label them and "call them names" but you seldom call them by their real name.)

1. Why did the act of giving the raccoons names change the way Jerry could treat them?

2. Read Matthew 16:17-18. Why did Jesus change Simon's name (Note: Peter means rock in the original language)? Is a name really significant? Does the fact that Jesus does the naming make it significant? Explain.

3. Read Revelation 2:17. In light of your answers to question #2 what does this verse suggest about your value, significance and uniqueness to God? If you take this verse to heart, how will it impact the way you see yourself and the way you relate to others?

4. You're not going to like this question, but I have to ask. Is it possible that God has "named" those people who really irritate you? If so, you may as well start praying for them instead of plotting against them.

CHAPTER 10: THE GIFT

(RE: April 4, 2008)

April 4, 2008: the last day of Easter break for the school children of Kogoya. Even so, usually one or two hundred kids mingle here at the Hope Center, in Malawi, Africa about an hour and a half outside of Blantyre. One of my tasks is to write a letter from each of 340 kids to their individual sponsors back in the states. Usually Catherine translates for me while I type on this laptop, which now appears eight years older than it did two weeks ago. Sometimes I hire a few college students to write letters on some tablets I picked up at the market.

Today all of the children present had already dictated their letters. So we played some games I made up. After a while I discovered that none of them knew the math symbols for greater than or for less than. Having no translator, I finally got the concept across. Then I wrote in symbols that zero is less than x which is less than 100. I then pointed to one bright young boy who guessed five. I wrote x is greater than five. I then pointed to another and she said six. So I symbolically wrote x is greater than six. I then called on one boy who had a twinkle in his eye. He jumped to ten. Then another jumped to twenty. Finally they got a less than and more saw what was happening. When I wrote an equal sign between the x and their guess, I led them in a cheer.

They could hardly contain themselves for the next game. Of course for the next game I used y instead of x. They got it a little sooner, so I pointed that out to them. By then their one meal of the day was ready. To my amazement, not one of those playing the game left. They knew they could get their lunch a little later. (The exact opposite would have happened the last time I was here, in 2005.) I wrote zero is less than z, which is less than a thousand. They laughed at what seemed too big a task, but continued and soon had my number.

After a while, a translator came and I also knew this game had to end so they could eat. I picked the boy with the twinkle in his eye to go write a number between zero and a thousand on a tiny piece of scrap paper. We put the paper in my pocket and I began to guess his number. Of course, my first guess was five hundred. The boy smiled and simultaneously ducked, as he could not believe I had gotten it on the first try. When I took out the paper and showed it to everyone they cheered. They must have thought I was some type of wizard. So I picked another boy to try. I put the small piece of paper in my pocket and wrote down my guess, five hundred. He signaled smaller, so I wrote the less than symbol between the variable and the five hundred so all could see. My next guess was, naturally, two hundred fifty. The boy smiled and simultaneously ducked; as he could not believe I had gotten it on the second try. I wonder if I should show them how to pick "devious" numbers in the future.

That night, Bill Saunders and I went to dinner/devotion in Mfumwe (pronounced voom way). Imagine about a dozen people in a room singing perfectly, beautifully, harmonically in a language you didn't understand, but knew they were singing about the love of Jesus. It is something one does not easily forget. The only tune we recognized was "The Old Rugged Cross."

I had been asked to give the devotion and decided to tell the story called "The Day the Gift Came." Here it is in case you do not know it.

Julia was born in Rochester, New York in 1911. When she was still very little she contracted Rheumatic fever. The doctors said she would probably not live to see her teens. One can only imagine what it must have been like for her parents to live with that knowledge. But as it turned out she lived long enough to marry and to see each of her children marry. When one of her daughters or daughters-in-law announced an impending birth she would make a pair of booties for the baby to wear home from the hospital. She and her husband had six children and twenty-one grandchildren before he died in 1976.

Two years after he died, Julia grew increasingly breathless even after just a short walk to her nearby mailbox. The option of heart surgery came up and she said that if the surgery were successful it would be good because she could pick up her "honey-bunnies" (grandchildren) again. If the operation were not "successful" she would be with the Lord, so either way it would be good.

When the doctor met the family after surgery, he told them that stitching her heart was like trying to sew "wet tissue paper." Her heart just kept falling apart. She died several hours later, but as she said, it was good.

Six years later my sister, Marilyn, came over for a visit. My wife, Adele, was due in two weeks with the little girl who would turn out to be our only child. As Marilyn was preparing to leave, she handed me a gift. It was a pair of booties for our baby to wear home from the hospital. Handmade by my mother...Julia! The sudden awareness of somehow feeling loved again by someone that no longer lives on earth opened a torrent of wonderful memories.

I am not certain how long it took before I realized this was not the first time I had received a beautiful gift from someone who had died. Jesus had willingly given his life to pardon each of us from all the wrongs we have committed.   Jesus loves us regardless of what we have done. Our job is to simply accept the gift.

Before we left I thanked the group for singing "The Old Rugged Cross," the hymn that had been the favorite song of my mother.

Jerry

DISCUSSION/REFLECTION QUESTIONS

CHAPTER 10: THE GIFT

0. Think of a special gift you have received. Do your best to recall how it made you feel when you first got it.

1. What makes a gift meaningful to you: the cost of the gift, who gave you the gift, the thoughtfulness that went into selecting the gift or possibly something else?

2. When you receive an exceptional gift, how does that make you feel towards the giver? How does it make you want to act towards the giver?

3. Read Philippians 2:6-8 and Ephesians 2:1-10. What do these verses say about the cost and thoughtfulness of the gift of salvation, and about the person who gave us the gift?

4. What does your current lifestyle suggest about your appreciation for God's gift of salvation? What might cause you to under-appreciate God's gift? What can you do to appreciate it more?

CHAPTER 11   A NON-TYPICAL WEEK

(RE: c April 16, 2008)

If you are driving down a dirt road in Kogoya and see a thin
strand of weeds lying across the road (and a matching strip
around thirty to forty yards later) it means "slow down to one or
two miles per hour." If you are walking, it means "be quiet here,"
because there has been a death in one of the nearby huts. It is a
sign of respect. We have seen one of these places about every
three days since we came here. The latest one was for Ethelo
James, a young pregnant girl who was in our program here at the
Hope Center. She was having problems with her slightly
premature delivery and was taken to a nearby clinic late at night.
We deduced she was probably hemorrhaging, and a call made by
cell phone for transport to a larger hospital came too late.

Clement used the Miqlat truck to go buy a coffin for close to
3,000 Kwacha—or about $20. He drove Ethelo's body to the
cemetery as the mourners followed on foot. This scene has been
too frequent here.

Connex, a national on the Miqlat team, is buying a car on credit--
rather expensive. He lent it to his friend Richard so he could
take his fiancée home. No one was hurt when Richard rolled the
vehicle. Insurance will not cover the totaled car.

Bill and I are making good progress on the trusses and I have
only 65 students to go in the letter-writing department. Bill has
been driving us in a van borrowed from some great people who
run the Healing Hope Center, which we pass on the way to the
village. Although he is a little uncomfortable driving on the left
side of the road, he does a great job and is cautious. However, he
did break the front left shock absorber. Today, Friday, we found
that the cost of one factory shock was $600. We decided to go
non-factory. We, (Bill, Weston, and I) had planned to get an
early 8 AM start, but finding a shock took a long time.

While waiting at the office (part Miqlat office and part Christian Community Church office) Bill got some needed work done with Blessings Jim (his given first and last name.) Blessings Jim is our go-to guy at the village. I, on the other hand came across Samuel, a twenty-four-year-old having difficulty with some algebraic problems. He was shocked that I not only knew mathematics and found his mistakes, but that I did it while standing in front of him looking at his paper upside down. At one point the plan was to have Bill stay in the office while Weston and I went out to the village to work on the new building. Instead, the three of us left in Clement's Miqlat truck just after noon.

A few hours after we left, Pastor Gideon and Francis (the mechanic and a new Christian) took our newly repaired van for a test drive. Connex, Clement, Blessings, and sweet Gloria (the receptionist) stayed behind at the office and were caught by surprise when seven men armed with one shotgun and six pangas (short machetes) walked in. They brought Blessings from around back and marched him and Gloria into a back office with Connex, where they thought they would find a large sum of money. They had not yet seen Clement. They asked where the abusa (pastor) was. They wanted money.

They hit Blessings and Gloria on the head with the butt end of their knives. One asked, "Should we kill them?" Just after that, Clement was ushered into the room where all the victims were now lying on the floor. The armed robbers took their money and wallets, cell phones, two laptops with the backup flash drives storing two years' worth of records and work. They also took the checkbooks. There was a little more money in the office than normal for various reasons, but it was under $200. Normally they would have found two vehicles parked outside, but we had the truck and the borrowed van was on a test drive, so zero cars were taken.

The brazen gang of seven locked their victims in the barred office. Clement was eventually able to break through the roof and let the others out. It was good that Bill and I weren't there. They would have taken Bill's backpack with his passport and they would have taken this computer with most of the letters on it. Plus we would not have known what they were saying and who knows what they would have done to a couple of amazungu (rhymes with ah bazooka and means foreigners).

That night Francis (the mechanic) went to collect for a job he had done, but the wife said her husband was out drinking. Francis went to the pub to look for him; when the pub's patrons saw the church shirt he was wearing, two men ran out the door. He called the police, who came and arrested the two men (who did not run). We don't know much more yet.

Before we knew about the situation back at the office, we actually got a lot done. On the trip back, as usual, we told stories, planned, and laughed for most of the 80-minute trip. This time Weston drove the truck. We met Clement at the office a little after five and he gave us the preliminary report.

The main concern is psychological damage of those affected. Sorry for the terse writing, but we must eat. We are okay.

Jerry

DISCUSSION/REFLECTION QUESTIONS

CHAPTER 11   A NON-TYPICAL WEEK

0. Think back to a time you tried to calm someone who was frightened or upset. Were you successful? What could you do to be more effective in the future?

1. Have you ever experienced a near-death moment? What effect did it have on you? What, if any, changes did it cause in you? Did those changes last? Why or why not?

2. Read Psalm 39:4-6. What do these verses say to you? How do you feel after reading them? What lessons can you learn from them?

3. Read Matthew 6:25-34. On a scale of 1-10 how well are you doing at living the way Jesus describes in these verses? 1 = "Not even close, 10 = Worry free. What would it take to live the way Jesus describes?

4. Read Psalm 56. What gives David confidence? Do you live the way David describes? Explain. Trust is built when you take risks that require trust. What is one thing you can do differently to exercise more trust in God?

CHAPTER 12   OUT OF AFRICA INTO FALLBROOK
(RE: April 17 – 20, 2008)

About a dozen years ago, we met a sweet man we came to call Uncle Louie. He rented a studio from us for a few years. He always made me feel good. He said I had a great family and a special place to live. He moved away a few years later, but one of us would call the other about every month or two, just to catch up. He would always want to know how our daughter Laura was doing. He let me know he would like some pictures too. Two weeks before I left for Africa he called and said in his gravelly voice, "What's up, Big Jer?" I told him what I would be doing and he said he would pray for me. Isn't it great when someone offers to pray for you? He always makes me feel good.

Ever wished you had your camera (or cell phone), but didn't? Imagine five kids under the age of five walking from the village well to their huts, each balancing a filled jug on their respective heads. Imagine that one little girl's jug leaks and her three year old brother is walking behind and to the left of his sister with a bowl in an attempt to capture some of the escaping prize. Further imagine that the girl thinks the brother isn't doing a good enough job so she takes the bowl and in an effort to be more efficient tries to catch the water herself. She holds the bowl in her left hand and turns counterclockwise to capture the liquid, but as she turns, so does the jug on her head. Can't you just see the circle? Precious. That was one of the first memories I had on this trip.

The difference between the children of Goliat in 2005 (the last time I traveled there and helped make the trusses for the Hope Center) and those in the program in 2008 is stunning. Malnourished, barefoot kids running around in rags had been transformed into vibrant barefoot kids running around in rags. Eighteen months ago they were each given a new single set of clothes, doubling their collective wardrobes. A year and a half of twenty-hour use (literally) has taken its toll on buttons, stitching and cloth, but the health advancement is dramatic. What would you rather have: nice clothes, a nice shelter, or food? All three would be great, but if only one, we know which one.

In 2005 one such little boy took great care in observing whatever I did. He always wanted to hold my hand—a large contrast I suppose: tiny and black versus big and white. A few years later his hands were bigger, but he still had a smile and a curiosity as to what I would do. I mistakenly thought his name was Yamanya.

Things are just plain different over there. The crows have white breasts. Sort of looks like they are wearing tuxedos. (Reminds me of the Mike Hammer quote, "You can pin a bowtie on a penguin, but that doesn't make him Fred Astaire.") People drive on the left, no problem. In town they have roundabouts; a good idea! There was one intersection with a signal, but the lights were not actually visible. Everyone knew it did not function properly, so drivers just sort of looked at each other and then finally moved. Over a set of railroad crossing lights an official, well-made sign read, "These lights do not work."

And marriage...in the villages, when a girl reaches the age of about 14, (remember, many have no idea how old they are) and a boy would like to marry her, he just lets her know. If she agrees, she just says, "Yes." (And girls from poor families usually jump at the offer.) A village elder comes and gives some counsel, they tell people they were married, and that is it. If the girl really does not wish to marry, she may say, "No," but if the family is poor, the young girl will probably be talked into accepting.

Funds for mosquito nets were raised mainly due to the threat of malaria. Since several children had no blankets, special funds were procured for that too.

I am not certain if Catherine's accent, my hearing, or a combination of the two caused the problem, but sometimes understanding one another was tricky. I remember one time when I asked if the child for which I was writing had a favorite Bible verse or Bible story, Catherine clearly answered, "Ruthey." She saw me type Ruth, so again she said, "Ruthey." I said, "That is how we spell Ruth." We went around again, so she finally slowly said, " No, Lukey!" I said, "Oh, Luke." We both laughed.

My two main responsibilities were to help build ten trusses and write a letter from each child to his or her sponsor. On the last day, Bill had another meeting, so Weston and I drove out to the center and I made the last two trusses. As for the letters, I had all but two done. That day one of the two missing children was at the center, so I finished her letter. As were we leaving the center for the last time, we drove to the home of the last child. I wrote the letter on this laptop out in the "middle of nowhere."

One leg of our trip home was a scheduled 19 hour, 20 minute flight. Sitting at a window seat, I could see the full moon. From six miles up I could witness the ocean and then the cloud cover all illuminated by our earth's sole satellite. Since we were traveling almost due west at about 500 MPH on what is close to a sphere spinning toward the east at very nearly 1000 MPH (at the equator anyway), the moon only set at half speed. I had a personal view of a large section of our planet. I wondered if anyone else on the plane knew we could observe the full moon for twice as long that night. I wondered if anyone else in the sky was enjoying the tremendous earthscape.

On the other side of this earth there is a continent called Africa containing a country called Malawi. In that country there is a bustling city known as Blantyre. And about 42 clicks from there is a district called Thyolo (long 'o"s, Cholo); within Thyolo lies a collection of villages known as Goliat. One of those villages is Kagoya. And near its centroid is a rise on which stands a cookhouse, an almost completed clinic/library/tutorial building, and a huge hall called the Hope Center where 340 orphans can have a huge meal six days a week. One of those children named Namanya (with an ever-present smile) stopped by every several minutes just to see what I was up to.

Having left and returned during a full moon, I still, somehow, felt different to be home. Besides family news, I literally only knew two things from the states: Charlton Heston had died and Kansas had won the NCAA Basketball Tournament. I walked in

our barn door of a front door, set my stuff down and looked at
the flashing light of our phone's answer machine. It held a
beautiful, heartfelt message from a son saying his father, "Uncle"
Louie, had died.

DISCUSSION/REFLECTION QUESTIONS

CHAPTER 12   OUT OF AFRICA INTO FALLBROOK

0. Describe the last time you were in complete awe of
   something/someone.

1. Read Psalm 8. Have you ever felt this way? What makes you
   most aware of the wonder of God? Can you describe how you
   feel in those moments?

2. How might your life be different if you were more aware of
   the wonder of God?

3. How might your view of death be different if you were more
   aware of the wonder of God?

4. If you are a follower of Christ, what is something you can do
   as a daily habit to make yourself more aware of the wonder of
   God's presence in your life?

CHAPTER 13   PICTURE THIS

April 30, 2008

Use your imagination to see yourself as having been born
somewhere in Africa. Imagine you now live in a modest 10 x 12
foot hut you made from mud and plants found nearby.

A tiny, dilapidated American shack in your village would be the
largest and best house for miles. A hut with a piece of furniture?
Extra special. With glass in the windows? Extravagant. With
cold running water? Unbelievable. With a non-dirt floor? A
mansion. With a functional electric bulb? Sheer luxury.

One day some amazungu (non-derogatory Chichewa word for
"whites") drive up in a gollymoto (vehicle). You have heard of
amazungu, but have never seen one. They talk of putting in a
new well. Going for water means lengthy daily trips through the
many turns on the footpaths in the maize fields. Think how
blessed you would feel if some missionaries put in a new well just
200 yards from where you lived.

The young couple next door has a baby, and as is typical, the
father rarely, if ever, picks it up. Except when the infant is
sleeping or nursing, the mother keeps it tied tightly to her back
with a thin blanket. The baby does not get much action, day after
week after month after year.

If you could truly imagine that, you are good.

Knowing all this, one day before we started building trusses, Bill
said, "I bet if you put your arm around any one of those kids,
they will stay right there until you move away." Over the next
few weeks Bill and I tried it repeatedly. I believe his hypothesis
to be true.

Picture this scene: (As usual, I will do my best to tell it as it
actually happened.)

Around 6:30 am on the second day of a trip to Africa, in a big clearing, about twenty children are just hanging around. One might think it resembles a park in the states, except for the fact that all the Africans are barefoot and all the Californians wear shoes. And you see no sidewalks, or drinking fountains, or trash cans, or playground equipment, or parking lots, or grandstands, or covered areas, or picnic tables, or flush toilets, or sinks, or grass.

In this setting two cultures were represented and most were playing together with a solitary Frisbee. People laughed at how it could sail and how some could seem to make it go exactly where they wished. It was even fun when someone who had never seen or touched a Frisbee tried to throw it, followed by the inevitable chase after the errant disc. The Frisbee was a prize. The person who held it was the temporary center of attention and then got to work on tossing skills. All could see that some west coasters were rather accomplished with this half-century-old game. One young American was skilled enough to eat while holding his sandwich with one hand and catching and throwing the Frisbee with his other.

That certain young American caught the platter yet again and quickly tossed it off with his right hand while he absent-mindedly flipped the last bit of his sandwich to the ground with the other. And that marked the sudden and unexpected end of the game of Frisbee catch. No one went after the Frisbee. No one. Everyone sans shoes went straight to the crust lying in the dirt.

DISCUSSION/REFLECTION QUESTIONS

CHAPTER 13   PICTURE THIS

0. Have you wished or prayed to have a burden lifted? Many, maybe most, Americans do just that. In Africa they pray for help to cope with a burden. They pray for guidance to help them endure. Are you searching for some type of cosmic magic to make problems vanish or are you searching for guidance?

1. How rich are you? Go to the website www.globalrichlist.com to discover where you rank amongst the world's population. What do you think of the results? Do you feel rich? Why or why not?

2. Read 2Corinthians 9:6-11. What do you think, has God enriched you in every way? Give reasons for your answers.

3. Can you give an example of a time you gave reluctantly and a time you gave cheerfully? What made you reluctant? What made you cheerful? What motivates cheerful giving?

4. Have you ever truly appreciated and thanked God for the fact that your house has a floor? Or windows? Or a toilet? Or...? How do you show God your appreciation? According to 2Corinthians 9, how does God want you to show your appreciation? Can you trust God enough to take that kind of action?

CHAPTER 14   THREE FOR FIVE

(RE: June 5, 2008)

On Thursday, June 5, 2008, at around 1pm, I noticed a tiny ache. On a scale from zero to ten (zero being bliss and ten being whatever you are thinking is the opposite of bliss) I figured my ache was a zero point two. Something hardly worth mentioning, except it centered at my heart. Having had two heart attacks, each thirty minutes after a treadmill stress test, the pain worried me a little. I hoped it would go away. That night we had a men's group meeting, as we always do here on Thursdays. I figured I would go through the meeting and assumed it would just float away. I thought I would go to bed after the meeting and surely by morning things would be back to normal. I had made arrangements with Loren, from the men's group, to watch Lord of the Rings, The Two Towers (extended edition) in the morning.

I decided that if the ache remained after the movie, I would do something. Keeping the promise I had made to myself, I called the Kaiser advice nurse. He had me put nitroglycerin pills under my tongue. A few minutes after the third pill, the pain went away, but he said I had to go to the emergency room anyway, and that if it got worse to pull over and call 911. He said under no circumstances should I drive. I called Loren again and asked him to take me over. I put on the new Bermuda shorts I had purchased the previous week in Orlando after a bottle of spray sunscreen went off in my suitcase and emptied itself onto portions of several pieces of clothing. (It does not wash out. Adele had put it there because her bag was over the weight limit. But that doesn't top my going for a swim with my cell phone in my pocket, does it?)

While waiting for Loren, I thought how I would miss the retirement party for Tom T. that night and how I would also probably miss the meeting I was to lead the next morning. Time marches on with or without us.

When we arrived at Palomar Emergency they checked me in

pretty quickly and I had an EKG, a blood draw, and an x-ray. While walking through the hallways I saw Maddy, a friend and nurse there. She stopped by later to catch up.

They put me in a curtained room in the ER. I was waiting for results of the blood test for enzymes that would indicate I had had a heart attack. I guess the hospital staff was juggling patients; people on gurneys lined the hall. I had brought "The Chimes" (our church monthly) to read. I finished it and then read the stuff on the walls while lying on my gurney. (Did you know it is a good idea to wash your hands frequently and that vegetables are our friends?) Now I had nothing to do but wait. And wait. The monitor behind me showed several things. First, it reported the percent of oxygenated red blood cells passing through the capillaries of my right index finger. Second, it kept tabs on my heart rate. On the former, anything above 91 is good. Mine was 98. I figured out that I could increase my lung efficiency to 100% if I took deeper breaths. I determined I could decrease my HR if I concentrated on relaxing. But I could not do both at the same time. I finally solved the puzzle by making my stomach go up and down instead of my chest while breathing. I was bored, but not uncomfortable or ungrateful.

Through a four-foot opening in the curtain, I could view others. I could see and hear many things. A 28-year-old man had broken his wrist in a fifteen-foot fall on the job. I could see from his neck to his work boots. He had no shirt on--and was skinny. To the left of him I heard a 29-year-old man who had been hit by a car while on his motorcycle. I could see neither him nor the sheriff to whom he was speaking.

In the room to my left was the most interesting man of all. He had awakened with double vision and was telling his life story to a lady who I assume was an admitting officer. He had had some lymph nodes in his groin removed and a cancerous tumor on his sphincter misdiagnosed as a hemorrhoid for two years.

Then it happened; for the second time in three months I so wished I had been video taping. A silent scene passed across the opening in the curtain in about six seconds. First I heard a gurney approaching from the left. Then I saw the man lying on his back. As he passed, I saw his butch haircut, his huge white T-shirt, his blue-jean knee-length shorts, his white socks and white with black tennis shoes hanging over the end of his temporary bed on wheels. He must have been at least 6' 5" and 350 lbs. (funny the abbreviation is lb. and neither letter is in pound). He was followed closely by two women, probably his wife and sister. None of this is too remarkable. It is what lay on his stomach that made it such a memorable tableau. A boy, maybe three or younger, held onto his father as a baby monkey clings to the belly of his mother as she swings from handhold to handhold. The exhausted boy was sleeping, his mouth open and his expression peaceful, content, and secure. His father was in trouble, but even in sleep the son was not about to let go.

Later they brought me to Room 623. I donned the traditional hospital patient apparel and followed instructions, which included taking a pill and some Pepcid to help with an upset stomach, which I did not have, and peeing in a bottle. (A few minutes after taking the pill, sure enough, my stomach became a little queasy, but it went away when the pill wore off.) Meanwhile, Dale called to let me know he had turned off the river fountain outside at my house, which I had left on.

The results came in from the blood work; I did not have an attack. So I would probably have a stress test the next day.

Saturday morning I noticed that all the people in the ward were old, except me. I'm fifty-eight. I was the only one with one of those IV stands on wheels that I had to take wherever I went. They wheel-chaired me to the imaging room and parked me outside the door in the hallway, facing a lady who was probably in her early nineties. There we were, face to face. So what else could I say but, "Come here often?"

I informed the doctor administering the test that I was 2 for 4 on stress tests followed by a heart attack. He determined from the EKG printout that I had a rate-related left bundle branch block. (Say that 58 times in a row.) He explained that my heart received electrical signals to beat at a low rate via a certain path, but that path would change for higher rates. (You can plug your radio in at the kitchen; you can plug it in at the garage; either way you get commercials.) This, coupled with the fact that sometimes my heart is fed by traditional coronary arteries and at least two other times by smaller collateral arteries I had grown as a teenager, scientifically proves that my wires really are crossed and that is why I am the way I am. (Send donations through www.whoisthisguyreally.com.)

After half an hour I did not have an attack, so I am now three for five. I showered and waited for the results of the images taken before and after my stress test.

I told Adele not to come to the hospital from her horse show, since she could do nothing but look at me in my flowered boxers anyway. Bill and Judy volunteered to take me home. I am used to having Bill drive me around; he did it for a month in Africa. I called them and got dressed while they were on their way. The nurse had already disconnected all the electrical leads and I was sitting on the bed, all set except for signing out and the removal of the one and one-quarter inch IV needle sticking in a vein on the back of my left hand. She was meticulous in the removal of all of the tape and stuff, which kept it in place. Then for some strange and unknown reason, she rapidly removed the needle, but not back out along its axis as it had gone in the day before. She pulled it out at an awkward angle, causing blood to go onto the sheets and my brand new shorts, but fortunately for me, mostly onto the sheets.

On the way home Judy asked me how I slept. I said I slept off and on, but woke up the exact number of times that I fell asleep. This should be a goal for everyone. They dropped me off and I went in to find many messages on the machine. (My cell phone battery had drained to one bar, so I had turned it off most of the time to save juice.)

Then I noticed the kitchen timer I had set to remind me to turn off the river pump (out at the play house). Dale had checked things for me and had turned off the pump. I wasn't home to

hear it go off 32 hours 51 minutes 17 ... 18 ... 19 seconds...
ago. Time marches on with or without us.

DISCUSSION/REFLECTION QUESTIONS

CHAPTER 14   THREE FOR FIVE

0. The little boy clinging to his father felt safe. Where are some places you feel completely and fully safe?

1. How do you feel when you have moments like Jerry's when reality hits you once again that life really goes on without you?

2. Read Psalm 131. What allows David to feel content? Could an experience like Jerry's bring that kind of contentment? Why or why not?

3. Read Romans 12:3 and then 1 Peter 5:5-6. Why is humility an important and necessary character trait for a follower of Christ? Why is humility important to God? In what ways has Jesus shown humility?

4. In what ways do you show humility? When are you most likely to not show humility? What action step can you take to develop the character trait of humility?

CHAPTER 15   ON TRACK

(RE: June 21, 2008)

A few days ago, Saturday, June 21, 2008, some of us were at the Fallbrook track helping raise money for cancer research through a twenty-four hour event called "Relay for Life." So I thought I would tell a track story or two.

Each season before our first big track meet, I would give a speech introducing a scenario whereby the final event, the mile relay, would determine the meet's victor. (We made certain every person on our team knew how to perform a mile relay handoff.) It was the perfect time to review some of the things they had practiced. I would then describe a race where our last runner got the baton and was behind. It did not matter by how far. Pumping my arms with shoulders high and fists tight, I would demonstrate how our runner (I would name a team leader) would not say through clenched teeth and in an excited voice, "I'm gonna get that guy!"

"No," I emphasized, "that is not what he will do. He will secure the baton, and say..." and then in a cool, calm, confident, deep voice I would say, "I'm gonna get that guy." Shoulders down, wrists relaxed, jaw loose, expending energy, but not fighting his own body.

During the season I demonstrated different running styles (no two bodies are the same) and let the team try them out. Running with the forearms basically always horizontal, like a train, was not good for acceleration, but possibly excellent for maintaining speed with less exertion. Some used it on the first straightaway of a quarter mile race. A different technique was to run as if reaching for something in front of you and then throwing it away behind you. Another required concentrating on flicking the heels on each stride, especially if you felt yourself slowing. This would increase everyone's stride length while not affecting their rate much, so it made some slightly faster because speed is a combination of stride length and stride rate.

One shy young man, Tom "Bucky" Buchfeller, just could not adapt to any of these techniques. While never poetry in motion, he was all heart—someone any coach would want on the team. To help him, I made up a drill for the whole team to try. When they ran on a straightaway, I asked them to look at the shadows of their heads compared to a long line on the ground and see if they could find a way to make their shadows bounce less.

My fourth year as head coach was in 1981. By the last dual meet of the season, all three of our teams were undefeated. The Girls' team and JV Boys' team were set on paper to win (and they did), but the Varsity Boys were looking at a squeaker with the also undefeated Arlington Lions. Their best athlete, Chris Harper, was injured and our best sprinter (the previous year's league and CIF champion, Greg Thomas, who would have been the state champ in most states) was also injured. Winning the meet came down to the mile relay. Five points for first and zero for second. The winners of the relay would be the league champs. They decided to put Harper in the relay and my team asked me to put in Thomas, but I knew that would not be good for him in the long run. So we would run Rich Teel, Silas Hale, and "Bucky" in for our fastest quarter miler, Thomas. Chris Crisman (who a few weeks later would run the fastest time in the nation in the hurdles) would bring home our baton. Funny I remember the names after all these years.

Unlike other track teams, we had a rule that everyone stayed until the end of the meet. During the running of the JV and Girls' mile relays, I had our team spread themselves evenly around the inside track (running alongside a participant is illegal). The opposing Lions saw what we were doing, but were now outnumbered by Bears all the way around their own track. I told our first three runners we just needed to give our anchor the lead. Inside I was hoping for at least fifteen or twenty yards. Rich and Silas ran with the fluidity they had practiced all season. Although expending energy, they ran relaxed, with all effort placed into forward motion. Silas had a slight lead coming in, but he and Bucky picked up a couple of yards more on the exchange. Bucky ran on guts and will and came in with a seven-yard lead. After the final exchanges, we had a ten-yard lead.

(Overall, it doesn't matter how fast the runners run, it matters how fast the baton travels).

Ten yards isn't much in a quarter mile race, and everyone knew it. The two anchors were running while the athletes ringing the track, the fans in the stands, and the coaches on the field cheered. Lions were yelling, "Chris. Chris. Chris." for Chris Harper, while the Bears were hollering, "Chris. Chris. Chris." for Chris Crisman. The voices synchronized. It was electric. I will not forget the volume of the unified chant, the sight of the two Chrises running in line ten yards apart, or what happened at the end. I was down on the infield, about thirty yards from its center. I typically recorded each runner's individual split. Well, not this time. I just watched. The ten yards between the runners never shrank, never increased.

The Bears won by ten yards. That was the only season I wore a hat, a straw cowboy hat given to me by my mother-in-law. I actually threw it in the air. It was not pandemonium. It was proof of hard work paying off which led to confidence-building school pride -- the good kind of pride. When things settled Bucky came over and stood directly in front of me. He didn't say anything; he just looked at me and smiled. I wanted to rub his head as my father would have, but I looked him in the eye, smiled back, and nodded. Things changed that day, in ways I couldn't have imagined at the time...and not just for Bucky.

A few years later the Arlington head coach, John Corona, confessed to me, "I don't like to lose, but it is not quite as bad when it is to you."

A quarter century after that race, just outside of the Riverside City College stadium I was talking with my good friend and long-time campus aide for Poly High, Tim Klock. I was getting ready to announce one of my last football games for the Bears. I heard, "Coach! Coach Maurer." Toward me came Irick Hale, a hurdler for four years, including the team back in '81. He was a great kid who had a few learning problems back then. We spent some time catching up. I asked him about his older brother Silas, who had run the second leg on the mile relay, and little sister Lisa, each of whom were also on the track team for four years. Lisa now coached track at a college in Arizona, but Silas had died several years earlier of cancer. So young. I expressed my earnest regrets.

Before I left to prepare for the pre-game, Irick volunteered that being on the team all those years ago had changed his life. He said that the confidence he had gained had made him the man he had become. I looked at him and I looked at Tim. I think Tim knew what that meant to me. As we parted, Irick said, "Thanks, Coach." Little did he realize how much encouragement he had given to ME.

At the Relay for Life the opening ceremonies concluded with the starting lap of special T-shirt-wearing and banner-clad cancer survivors. As they walked their lap I noticed, as I stood behind our booth not far from the infield's center, that the small crowd began cheering. I figured that in about thirty seconds the honorees would be where no supporters stood along the course. I know a thing or two about cheering people on a track. I made my way over to the curve behind carnival-type booths and the castle-shaped Jumpity Jump Jump. I was the only one there. I could see that the co-leader and two-time cancer survivor was crying. She pointed to me and choked back, "Thank you, Sir." Soon other supporters ran to the curve to cheer. I saw other survivors weeping. Was it because they had survived? Was it because people were cheering that they had fought and won and now they were walking a victory lap? Was it because they were remembering what they had been through?

I continued clapping with all the others as they passed. Then I saw one of my really good friends from church, Mimi Leraas, with whom I had just been sitting and talking on the infield minutes before, walking the lap--a petite but dramatically emotion-packed being. This moment drove reality home: they had survived and others they knew had not. They had been through more than we knew. In that exact instant, the face of my sister Dixie came into my memory. She was one of the patients who did not get a banner, but I know in my heart she cheers for all who do.

All the onlookers who had come to the curve to cheer now went on ahead to the straightaway to continue to spur those walking. All except me. I stayed there behind the blue and yellow castle. I guess I didn't want anyone to see me crying, too.

DISCUSSION/REFLECTION QUESTIONS

CHAPTER 15   ON TRACK

0. Ever worked hard for something and won? Ever worked hard
    for something and lost? Try to imagine working hard toward
    a goal and it actually was a life or death race.

1. Do you see yourself as a cheerleader? Who in your life do you
    demonstratively cheer for? Who are the cheerleaders in your
    life who encourage you?

2. Read Hebrews 3:13 and 1 Thessalonians 5:11. Why is
    encouragement needed? What is the goal or purpose of
    encouragement? Would you describe yourself as an
    encourager? Would your family describe you as an
    encourager?

3. Read Hebrews 12:1-3. According to this passage (and the
    verses around it) who are the "witnesses" cheering you on?
    What is the race you are running? Who are you running for
    and how do you know if you are running well? Who can you
    surround yourself with to encourage you to throw off
    hindrances?

4. Who needs your encouragement? What can you say or do for
    them to encourage them? If you have children, what can you
    do to encourage each one today? What can you do to
    encourage your parents today or your spouse? What can you
    do to encourage a friend this week? What can you do to
    encourage your pastor this week?

CHAPTER 16   MY BEST FRIEND MIKE

(RE: 1963 -)

Summer 1963: I had recently graduated from Bloomington Junior High School. So had one Michael J. Pound, but we had never met. One afternoon we were each independently walking toward the other in a covered, exterior hall of an otherwise deserted campus called Alpha Lyman. I don't remember who said hello first. I *thought* we were both amazingly shy back then. I don't know how many months or years it took me to figure out that Mike wasn't really shy. When asked a question, he rarely answered within two seconds. In fact, more like six seconds would elapse before he responded with his thought-filled reply. "Think before you speak," the old adage goes. Mike should have been the ad man for that great piece of advice. Ask him a hard question and he would consider the many possibilities he could pursue and tacks he could take, shift his current physical position, and finally reply with his best. Ask him an easy question and he would do the same thing.

We became friends, then best friends. We would play catch for hours, sometimes not saying a word. At first we threw the football. I would run a pattern and he would throw. Then I would stop and from right there he would run a pattern and I would throw. Sometimes we would go for long periods and the ball would not touch the grass. When we became too tired to run, we would switch to throwing a baseball. Less running. Mike always gave his best, in practice, in the game, in life.

After a few years in high school football, I dropped out of that sport for two reasons: first, I was chicken, and second, I wasn't any good. That did not stop our playing catch, but eventually Mike ran 80% of the patterns, while I threw harder and harder and harder. (I guess our natural aptitudes prevailed.) When we were sophomores, they had every boy throw a softball for distance, and I won. Two years later, not only was Mike the fastest man in school, he was the fastest 220 sprinter in the Citrus Belt League.

During our junior year, Mike talked me into going out for track. Mr. Claude Johnston (the teachers called him Bud) coached pole vault, and Mr. Bill Rogers coached everything else. I remember a drill the whole team would do. It would prove to be the best drill not only for me, but for my many teams in the future. Coach Rogers would say, "Go do ten build-ups". Bear with me here. It is a 100-yard drill. You start on one goal line walking, loose and relaxed and easy. Slowly and gradually you increase your speed, but maintain your loose and easy attitude, never ever gritting or straining. You gradually go through the different speeds of walking, jogging, running and sprinting. If you did it correctly, in the last 15 to 30 yards you were running faster than you had ever run in your life, you were spending a great deal of energy, but were not straining or fighting yourself. You were still relaxed and loose with all of your energy going into forward motion.

You were supposed to do this drill with at least one partner. Mike and I would always run together and sometimes someone one else would join us. During our junior year we were a perfect match until about the 75-yard mark, whereupon I would reach terminal velocity and Mike would pull away. I suggested to Mike that maybe he should run this drill with someone else because I was holding him back. He said that he enjoyed running with me and that I had never held him back. Inside, I felt it did.

In his senior year, Mike came into his own on the football field as a wide receiver for our Bloomington Bruins. Great speed and even better hands. His routes were consistent and tight, many of us figured that he would get more scholarship offers than anyone else.

On a different front, I zeroed in on a mathematics contest between several Southern California High Schools. The top three math students from each school were to vie as a team for school honors. I thought I was good by getting good grades and all A's in math. Mike, however, got all A's in all things! Mike was number one, I was number two, and John Rykavic (another straight A student and our football team's quarterback) was number three (as ranked in our common senior math class.) We just *knew* that we would put Bloomington on the map... until Coach Phelps found out we might not get back in time for the football game. So, Mike and John were pulled. I became number one and Betty Sue Ward and Geeta Fobian became numbers two and three. We did okay, I guess, but we didn't put Bloomington High on the map.

A few Fridays later in a home game (played at nearby Colton High) Mike ran a down-and-in pattern. The ball was a little high, so he jumped and stretched to catch it. The safety running full speed in the opposite direction hit Mike head on. Both sides fell into silence after the collision. The ambulance silently rode onto the field. Mike never moved.

I didn't want to go see him in the hospital, but a little bit later Bill Collins and I entered his room. He looked so small and frail. I was wondering when he would get to play again, when I should have been praying for his life. He had a concussion, a devastating career-ending concussion.

Mike didn't come back to school for quite awhile. Some thought he was taking an awful long time to answer their questions, but then, they didn't know him very well. We didn't play as much football catch after that.

By the time track season came around, he was more than just ready to go. Mike was a little thinner now, but also a little faster. Now when we did our build-ups, we were still even most of the way, but before long he would pull away faster than before. Near the middle of the season however, something happened. I was almost staying with Mike at the end of our build-ups. I asked him if he was letting up. He said he wasn't. A little later we were even and a few times I would pull away by a few inches in the last ten yards.

For the first time, I guess, Coach Rogers probably thought Mike was dogging it. He told the second fastest kid, a tall, skinny junior who usually came in just a handful of yards behind Mike on meet days, "Run with Pound and Maurer." This was going to be different. The three of us stayed together through the walk, jog, and run portions, but as we slowly and easily moved into full speed, Mike and I left our young friend behind. That was fun!

As it turned out, I had the most fun in track during certain practices with Mike. Believe it or not, our landing pit for the high jump was sawdust held in by a "U" shaped, 18-inch high, solid wood fence. Mike did the Eastern role (the Fosbury Flop had not quite become popular yet). I had seen Mike take off from the left side, go up off his left foot, lead with his right knee, lay out, curl over the hard triangular metal bar, land on his back after a long fall onto the not-so-soft compressed sawdust, and have the wind knocked out of him. As you know, I was afraid of getting hurt, so I did the old fashioned scissors kick from the 1920's. I ran up almost parallel to the bar from the right side, jumped up off of my left leg, kicked up high with my straight right leg, then snapped down my right leg as I whipped my left leg over. I did not even need a pit; I landed on my feet and just walked out. Chicken!

One day, practice had ended, but Mike and I wanted to stay and practice high jumping. Coach said we could stay, but he asked us to bury the cross bar and two standards in the sawdust when we were finished because he had to lock the track shed some 200 yards away. For some reason, a large portion of the team hung around, probably to see how high Mike would go. After a while some of the guys said they would like to try it, so we set it very low. I said I could hurdle that. And someone bet that I couldn't. So I did. Then Mike suggested to all that we see who could hurdle the highest. Seemed like a good idea, so we moved the standards away from the pit onto the grass of the football field and one by one we gave it a shot. You had to run in a perpendicular path to the bar, jump over somehow, land on the other side and keep on running. One miss and you were out, but if it was deemed that you might make it on a second attempt, you could jump again.

We tried one at a time, re-setting the cross bar whenever we missed. Most of us made the first height. Moving the bar up in two inch increments, we ran again and again. A made-up event? Yes, but we were just some guys having some fun back in 1967.

No one knew who was going to win; eventually it came down to Mike and me. Mike, a great runner and high jumper, and me, a would-be hurdler and a would-be high jumper. Best friends just having another competition. Up two inches. Up two inches. Then Mike missed and I made it. Mike tried it again, but knocked it off. "Well," they said, "let's see how high Maurer can go." I finally missed at 4'10". Tried again, and missed. Mike said, "You hurdled 4'8"! You could jump over a Volkswagen!" That struck me. I could jump over a car! I should have figured out something about Mike and life right then and there, but a couple of years would pass before I would.

After we graduated from high school, Mike met Betty Hinkle. That changed things! But two years later, we were both attending Valley Junior College and Mike was a hurdler on the track team. As it turned out, we found a semi-shady spot on the track near the math and physics buildings. So I started joining Mike for his lone morning workouts twice a week. Soon we were back to challenging one another. I would set us off and whoever got his lead foot down on the other side of the first high hurdle won. Then we changed it to whoever got his lead foot down on the other side of the second hurdle won, and so on. After a few weeks, I started beating Mike, but only because I was the starter. So we began flagging down different people walking by to set us off. Usually Mike would win these races of varying length, but not always.

Gradually, I figured out an important truth. If you feel someone has confidence in you, it builds your confidence and you can do things you thought you could not. I also realized that Mike's confidence could be contagious. In high school, I had tried the hurdles for a while, but Coach Rogers had too much to do and I was chicken. Here, with Mike helping me and me helping Mike, we both got better and better.

I felt honored to be his best man the day he and Betty wed. Then he stood up as my best man when I married Adele. Then we had four girls. He had three and I had one. Mike won again! (All right, I know Betty and Adele helped.) Then we lived in different parts of California. We stayed in contact, but we just lived in different worlds.

He went on to do research in physics; I went on to teach math and coach football and track. We both had our share of victories. All those hours of throwing the football to Mike paid off when I coached receivers. After two years, I retired from coaching football.

My track teams ran build-ups. I ran hurdles with the hurdlers, and we ran to see who could get the lead foot down first on the other side of the hurdle. We had confidence. The last half of my head coaching career our teams were 72 and 3 with many league championships and CIF titles and a national mark in the hurdles. Confidence and influence can spill over and be soaked up by others.

I don't think either one of us liked speaking much, but Mike spotted for me the first several times I announced football games for Poly High in Riverside. I believe I improved. I was "the voice of the Bears" for twenty-seven years.

Several years later when our daughter Laura got to high school she earned thirteen varsity letters. One of the few events I missed was her first track meet. I could not believe that at her first meet she would be on varsity and run the hurdles. Hmmm, imagine that, the hurdles! Of course I did hear all about it that evening. The next morning I looked it up in the paper, and sure enough, in black and white: -- Laura Maurer, second in the varsity hurdles. First place from Poway High School was Audrey Pound. That's right; Mike and Betty's youngest daughter was a hurdler, too. We would see these two compete many times over the next three years; Audrey is one year older than Laura. The four girls still have marks in the record books at their high schools.

A few years ago Mike told us he had cancer. We watched him become frail, but he never stopped being Mike. I know what he gave me; I can only try to imagine what he gave his wife and daughters.

There are only three people who got to see both the wedding of his middle daughter, Jessica, and also Laura's wedding: Laura, Betty and me. Only Betty and I witnessed the two beautiful girls with their giant, warm smiles.

Betty stopped by the other day to give me a gorgeous tie pin made of silver and compressed roses from Mike's funeral. When I'm not wearing it, it sits just perfectly in a glass display case. Well, that isn't quite true. The beautiful pin that looks like onyx always sits in the glass display case; I can't bring myself to wear it.

DISCUSSION/REFLECTION QUESTIONS

CHAPTER 16   MY BEST FRIEND MIKE

0. Recall some best or great friends. Were you alike, or opposites?

1. When and/or where do you feel the most confident? What is the reason for your confidence?

2. Read 1 Samuel 17:32-53. What gave David his confidence? How did he develop it?

3. What suddenly gave the Israelite army confidence?

4. Faith leads to personal confidence and acts of faith can create confidence in others. What do you face that will require an act of faith? Where will you draw your confidence? Who might you inspire if you act courageously in faith?

CHAPTER 17 OF OLD CARS, NEW CARS AND CITRUS WAX

(RE: Oct. 2008)

Back in 2008 we were in the process of looking to sell a car and buy another. We would usually purchase a used car, but this time we were looking at a pre-owned. It's sort of complicated, but as I understand it, it is kind of like the difference between peeling a banana and skinning one. Well this made me consider what it must have been like to sell a horse, say, one point five centuries ago, with me being a marshmallow-hearted, hope-filled romantic and all. You couldn't tape a sign on the side of the horse and tie it somewhere on the outskirts of town for passersby to peruse. What would the sign say anyway? "Runs great, easy to ride, doesn't eat much, barn kept. Contact Jerrold at The Long Branch, evenings." This got me thinking how back in those days if you somehow became incapacitated but could just manage to hold on, there was a good chance old Buck could bring you back to the safety of home because he knew the way. (It is 150 years later but cars still can't do that.) I'm sure I saw this in some western somewhere. Maybe you saw that show too.

Well sir, it is a different age these days, so I went online to Craigslist.com and placed my "car for sale" ad. Whilst on Craigslist I decided to put a notice in the "Free" section regarding a few thousand oranges. We have fifty Valencia trees which should be picked around June. Usually some nice guys from the Senior Citizen's Center here in Fallbrook come and pick them, but months past the normal picking time the dwindling number of men who usually come pick hadn't. The trees already had the next year's crop part way in--not good for my old trees. In the ad I requested that a church group or NGO (a non-governmental organization,) come pick them, free.

About fifteen minutes after the ad posted, a lady named Lydia called and asked if I still had the oranges. I assured her I did and then asked if she was part of a church or NGO. She replied in the negative and wondered why I asked. I explained that I usually donate the entire crop and use the write-off to partially pay for the fertilizer and rather hefty water bill. She understood and said her goodbyes. Dozens of seconds later she called back with quite a sad story. She said she was just a poor single mother of five with no job, and her kids, "really loved to eat oranges." Could she just come and pick a few? Well, me being a marshmallow-hearted, hope-filled romantic and all, I was soon giving her directions to our ranch in the valley. She said she had a cell phone in case she got lost. Before hanging up I asked if she had a GPS. She said she did, so I told her to follow my instructions, since many GPS systems did not have this portion of N. Stagecoach Lane in them.

Lydia pulled up on time a few hours later in a car much nicer than any car we currently owned. She had her mother and two adorable little kids not yet old enough for school with her. Also, she appeared to be in the early stages of pregnancy. But, as every man can tell you, high on the list of the unwritten manhood rule book it says, "Never, ever, ask if a woman is pregnant." (I do believe it says that right below, "Eyes forward when at the urinal.") After I explained where and how to start picking, she took out an iPod with a tiny (TV) monitor built in and began listening to something.

Hmmm. She had a computer (to check my ad), a cell phone, a GPS, a nice car, and a new iPod...so was she poor? She thought she was (monetarily, at least). But she deserved kudos. She was raising her children herself. She actually did drive all the way out here and pick three big boxes of oranges in the high noon sun while possibly pregnant. I didn't know her story but she, unlike a growing number of others, did not quite seem to fit the concept of a bumper sticker I had seen months earlier, "Ask not what your country can do for you, demand it!"

When Lydia and her "helpers" finished she thanked me warmly and drove off happy, with a van full of family and citrus. She had not asked for money or help, just opportunity. What they used to call "The American Way."

Adele wanted to get a Lexus, while I wanted a Saturn, so we compromised and got a Lexus. When I flipped through the rather thick owner's manual, I saw one--and only one--page book-marked. It showed how to program a certain button above the rearview mirror to automatically open one's garage door. I pushed that button and the little red light came on, which I suppose meant it was working. This button could get me inside this car's previous owner's garage and from there I could almost assuredly walk right into their home. (The perfect crime!) But who knew where they lived? If only the car could take me home like old Buck. That is when I turned on the factory GPS, clicked "I agree" clicked "Destinations", clicked "My Locations", clicked "Go home", and there I saw the little carrier pigeon screen showing me how to go to its old home.

DISCUSSION/REFLECTION QUESTIONS-

CHAPTER 17 OF OLD CARS, NEW CARS AND CITRUS WAX

0. Have you ever imagined living in a different time? If you had to live in a different era, which would you pick and why?

1. Describe your most memorable experience of being lost.

2. Read 2 Corinthians 4:16-5:10. A nearly universal trait among humans is a feeling of dissatisfaction—a yearning for something more. What would Paul say is the reason for this yearning? Do you think that our yearning possibly points to the existence of God?

3. Why does Paul say we are confident? What are we confident about? How could this confidence influence the way we live? How would it influence the way we experience death? Is this true for you?

4. How do most people respond to their yearning for something more? Do you think their response is effective? How does Paul say we should respond and what reasons does he give?

CHAPTER 18   SECRETS

(RE: Sept. 1, 2008)

Can you keep a secret? Well over a year ago, Bill Saunders and I spent a month in Malawi, Africa. As you might imagine, we had occasion to converse on numerous topics. As you might further imagine, we spoke often of our families back home. We spoke of politics, abortion, the kids at the Hope Center, the administration of the project, his pictures and my letters, but the conversation always returned to our respective spouses, our kids, and his grandchildren. I remember Bill standing at attention, motionless, at the one spot on the compound where his old mobile phone got the best reception. Not very good reception, but good enough. Just so he could talk with his wife half a world away.

We spoke of how we met our wives and when we married. I remembered Bill and Judy's wedding year as soon as he said it, since it was just after my father passed away. One day we were talking about what we could do for our wives upon our return. I informed Bill that he would soon be married for one billion seconds. Some people might think, "Ho hum." But like me, Bill thought that was "kinda neat" and wondered when it would occur, exactly.

Well let me tell you, he asked the right man. I remember learning that there were 365 days in a year and 366 once every four years (leap year, Olympic year, and US Presidential elections). But my father always said it took 365.2524 days for earth to travel once around the sun (one Gregorian, tropical, or solar year.) For some reason, this fact stuck in my head. If a year were 365.25 days then every four years we would have precisely one "extra" day. If a year were 365.0025 days then every four hundred years would have one extra day. If a year were 365.2525 days, that would garner an extra day every four years plus one more extra day every four hundred years. But a Gregorian year really is 365.2524 days so years that are multiples of four are leap years except those which are multiples of 100 should not be unless they are also multiples of 400. (And that,

Ladies and Gentlemen, is partly why 1900 did not have a February 29 and 2000 did.)

Back to Bill's question, "When, exactly, will Bill and Judy be married one billion seconds?" I already knew the year of their wedding, so I merely needed the month and day: December 20. A little arithmetic and a little "Thirty days hath . . ." and I had it. September 1, 2008. Somehow we got the idea to have a one billion seconds anniversary party for the Saunders and make it a surprise for Judy. (I mean, she wouldn't be expecting a billion seconds party, would she?) We planned everything. I double-checked the date. It would be at our house, the Farmer and Adele's. A barbecue. I was hoping it would fall on a weekend, but it turned out to be a Monday. I triple checked: yep, September first, a Monday that, fortunately, happened to be Labor Day.

Once back in the states, we took care of details. Bill and I geocache, so Judy did not think anything of Bill's and my taking off to do stuff. We figured out whom to invite. We asked Wayne Taylor to BBQ the tri-tips and he said he would bring his special unit and take care of it; all we had to do was procure the meat. I did the math one more time before emailing the invitations for the Labor Day celebration at the Farmer and Adele's. Of course I had already warned every one except Judy to keep this a surprise for her. We planned everything.

As the day drew near, we had the official count of attendees. The idea, hatched in a different hemisphere half a year earlier, had grown feathers. Everyone but Judy knew about the surprise, but only a few knew we would be celebrating their billion seconds anniversary. Bill even had his speech down. This was going to be great.

Two days before the party, Bill told Judy we were going geocaching (a cover to do some party stuff). Is it okay to just lie like that? He brought the only suit he would ever own, the one in which he married Judy, and hid it in our closet. We then went to get the meat. We refined how we wanted things to go at the party while on the way. Bill said it didn't seem like a billion seconds since December 20, 1975. That was the year right before our country's bicentennial celebration, right before my father passed away.

Uh oh, I used the wrong year! All that checking with seconds, and I was off by precisely one entire year! So do I tell Bill his billion second anniversary was almost a year ago? Do I tell Bill that in two days, the day of the long awaited party, he will have been married exactly a billion seconds...plus one Gregorian year? I could tell the truth and take out the zing behind the surprise, not to mention Bill's big speech. I could just continue and keep the semi-depressing (to me anyway) secret to myself. A billion seconds plus one year becoming a special life marker is analogous to a couple of tubs of Jell-O and a shiny quarter becoming a workbench. I decided to keep the secret to myself and hope no one would check my simple arithmetic. Is it okay to just lie like that? A bunch of people fibbing (lying) to someone for a surprise party is one thing, but one person (me) lying to everyone is another.

The weather for the "Labor Day" party was excellent. Wayne and his sizzling-smoking Santa Maria tri-tip were situated by the arched gate. People got fresh popcorn from the popping cart by the Pop. 3, Elev. 552, Est. 1914, Tot. 2469 sign. It appeared to me that everyone was having fun as Bill went to don his marital garb. At a pre-arranged signal, I gathered everyone in the side yard and pretended to give a Labor Day speech. At this point Bill came walking up from the area of the east grove behind Judy. Most of us could see him. When Judy finally noticed something was happening, she turned to see her husband in his tan, corduroy, bell-bottomed, leisure wedding suit. At first she laughed, but after Bill looked at her and said, "A billion seconds ago *today*, I wore these very clothes when you made me the happiest man on earth. And I would like you to know I will love you for the next billion," she and everyone listening ... melted.

Except me. I already knew. And besides, it was a billion seconds plus one year. I wanted to see who would whip out some pocket calculator, or mobile phone, or PDA to check the length of a billion seconds in another time scale. No one did. We ate. We talked. We reminisced. Oh the pressure...all these friends thinking the Saunders wed 1,000,000,000 seconds ago, when I knew differently. I knew the truth. (The lie was eating at me.) Pictures were taken. Then more fun. More conversation, and then it happened. A guest, Bill H. (not to be confused with Bill Saunders, the man in the 31.6 year old suit) wanted to show me something on his Blackberry. I asked him to step over by the old oak, on the opposite side of the big swing, so no one could hear. Oh no. This was the moment I'd feared. But to my surprise he showed me something *unrelated* to my error. Nonetheless, I couldn't handle the pressure. I cracked. I explained my mistake and swore him to secrecy.

And now, all these seconds after that Labor Day, I come clean. I have kept the secret long enough. As the French say, "There is no pillow so soft as a clear conscience."

Jerry

DISCUSSION/REFLECTION QUESTIONS

CHAPTER 18   SECRETS

0. Everyone at the party kept the secret from Judy for quite a while. Bill and Jerry kept it for six months. Can you keep a secret?

1. Describe your favorite anniversary or birthday party. What made it memorable?

2. Read 1 Peter 4:8. What do you think Peter means? (If you have a commentary, look up this verse to see what a scholar thinks this means)

3. What is an example of being loved "deeply"? When was the last time you loved someone this way?

4. Make a plan to love someone deeply. Who will it be? By when will it happen?

CHAPTER 19   IRELAND

(RE: Feb. 2 – 9, 2009)

Recently a friend of ours said about Mexico, "Why would I want to go to a country where the good guys are afraid of the cops?" Another friend in another conversation said of France, "Too many Frenchmen are rude to Americans." But when Adele found a pretty good deal for a flight to--and condo in--Ireland, complete with car, we decided to go. People said, "The Irish are all so nice, and they love Americans, and you will love the food!" I suppose the only problem was we were leaving our own sunny Southern California for Ireland in February, the dead of winter. Maybe the timing made it a pretty good deal!

Our verdict is in: The Irish really are nice, all of them, really. During our week-long stay, we asked for directions a few times, and they would stop what they were doing, step outside if they were inside and do all in their power to assure we understood their directions. The entire country seems to be filled with kindhearted people. With the help of our GPS, "Emily," the four of us (friends, Russ and Jan, joined us) quickly found the facility in the county of Shannon that contained our condominium, but we could not find where to check in. We asked a young lady, Amanda, where we might find the office; she said to follow her. She drove her car to a hotel office. A few minutes later she drove to number 26, our three-bedroom unit.

Each evening we planned for the following day. We saw much: the cliffs or Mohr, Spanish Point, The Bun Ratty Castle, The Ring of Kerry, The Rock of Cashel (a Castle from the thirteenth century), Blarney Castle (no two-hour wait, as we only occasionally saw other visitors) numerous old churches and shops, and King John's Castle in Tiperary (Yes, that Tiperary. King John never actually made it to the castle, though he did send an emissary.) The Ring of Kerry was a stunning 112-mile drive around a large, circular-shaped and beautiful coastal chunk of land in South Ireland. We drove to Killarney and caught a bus for the tour. The views and day were spectacular with few clouds and virtually unlimited visibility.

One of the first things I noticed: each house looked freshly painted. At first I suspected some program to spruce up homes along the popular highways. But after several days on miles of highway and back roads, I ditched that idea. Almost *every* home had a meticulously neat paint job. Since Russ was driving and Jan was reminding him, "Left, drive on the left." And "Curb." And Adele was navigating with the help of Emily and foldable maps, I was fantastically free to observe the countryside and look for houses in need of paint. I actually found a few such homes, and pointed them out (like giving in to the urge to announce the sitting of dead animals to fellow travelers). There were not many such homes.

A short side note: In a small compartment of my suitcase I usually keep a tiny radio. I scanned through the channels. Some broadcast a Middle Eastern sounding language, but the other channels produced delightful Irish music, or someone speaking with that great warm, Irish brogue. We heard that accent everywhere, of course. In one store the cashier politely informed me of the total. While paying her in Euros, I noticed a coin and pointed out what someone had lost. She said I could have it. I answered, "Oh, the luck of the Americans." Her laugh, even more than her brogue, endeared her to us.

We cooked breakfast each morning in our kitchen, but ate lunch daily in whatever pub was suggested by some nice Irish person we met. We ate dinner nightly in some other pub. We visited many pubs. The food was good one time and great to superior the rest. While at the pubs, well, let's just say I've been known to pound down a beer or two. Actually that is true. I had a beer with a girl named Audrey after her company's volleyball game back in 1969 and then another with Bill Collins and the guys at a popular Pomona Pizza Parlor a few years later. So now it is three. Well actually the third was a stout, Guinness, at a pub called The Creamery, in Bun Ratty, Shannon, Ireland, right across the street from Bun Ratty Castle and Durty Nellie's in 2009. Tasted all right I suppose, but not as good as root beer. Root beer, now there's a drink!

After a great day in and around Bun Ratty Castle, which included an expansive, self-guided walking tour of surrounding exhibits and buildings, we decided on a late lunch at Durty Nellie's. A few minutes into our meal, a cheery group of about a dozen men joined our cozy area for chips and a draft. A nice young man whom I will call Pierre, sitting less than a meter away and on my right, started a conversation with me. We soon discovered they were all French, having just arrived for the big rugby match between France and Ireland the next evening. I said, "Oh, and for whom will you be cheering?"

We explained that one couple was from Illinois and another from California, whereby a second man whom I will call Jean, sitting way off to my right and cater-corner, said, while looking straight at Jan, "Excuse me, euw wu woi?" All laughed. Jan knew exactly what he meant and proceeded to enunciate: "Illinois." With a warm smile he tried to repeat it a few times and the collective group had a nice laugh. Then Jean said to the four Americans, "Say," and then he said what I presume was the first part of a hard to pronounce name. After a beat of silence, I repeated it. Then he said the full name and I repeated that. He raised his eyebrows and nodded his head at me. (Of course, I thought I had repeated it spot-on, including mimicked tonal inflections, but you'll have to ask Adele, Jan, or Russ about that. Although an infamous singer, my general pronunciation might be pretty good, possibly from hearing my father's rich Dutch accent, a few years of Spanish, and/or announcing thousands of names over the decades.)

Pierre, still on my right, politely asked me about the overall perception Americans had of the French people. Immediately I knew this was a time for diplomacy, but I also wished to remain truthful. I said, "Although I have never been to your country, I have heard others say many Frenchmen are nice, but others look down their noses at those who do not speak French."

More friendly conversation ensued, including—when asked by the Frenchmen--our opinions of Obama. Then a third Frenchman, whom I shall call, Claude, sitting across from me and adjacent to Jan, asked the four of us if we could name the current French prime minister. Silence emanated from our corner. In my mind I could see the diminutive man, but no name came to mind. More silence. I felt as if Claude was testing us. Finally I said, "I can't bring his name to mind, but he has that beautiful girlfriend." They all cheered and one of them said her name, and they cheered some more. Claude said a few non-memorable things followed by, "That is the problem with Americans; they don't even know the prime minister's name." (I wanted to mention that there was a county a few kilometers from our house that was bigger than France and had superior wine, but I did not.) No one had said the answer yet. The question was still out there as a challenge. (We know leaders, yes we do. We know leaders, how about yoooou?)

I was feeling the pressure, so I took a chance. I looked Claude in the eyes and said, "Can you name the prime minister of Finland?" Silence. More silence. Golden silence. Claude squirmed. Outside I was James Bond; inside I was Robin Williams (Yeaaaaahhhh.) (Oh Claude, if only you could be more like Pierre!) His countrymen made taunting and kidding noises toward Claude. Within seconds, various good-natured conversations erupted in the room and then Claude looked at me and started rattling off names. I suppose they were the last names of heads of state of various European Union countries. I nodded in agreement, but it did not matter. He did not know the name of the head of state of Finland.

Then a girl in a formal dress (probably prom night) walked passed the doorway to our world and the French cheered in unison. Jean momentarily stood and cheered. Jean started a tune, the US national anthem. The French joined in . . . Na aa na na na na, na na na na na na? Na... They all sang loud, and smiled, and some waved their pints in the air. I sang the words, but it all blended together. At the conclusion, Jean asked if we knew the French national anthem. (Here we go again: We know national anthems, yes we do! We know national anthems, how about you?) To which Jan (one of us Americans) sang: Dut duh da da da da da daaaaaaaaa duhda da... causing Jean to rise again and place his hand over his heart as all the French joined in for the notes that followed. Jean raised his brows, motioned his glass of dark stout toward Jan, and said, "Yes, she knows it!"

Too soon, the time came for them to continue their travels, a long way to go, and many pubs to visit. We wished them luck and a good time, and they responded in kind as the principals shook each of our hands. The last one out was Jean. He replenished his glass from the dregs of his party's glasses. (Oh Jean, why can't you be more like Pierre?)

That evening, Adele and I walked 300 meters to the hotel lobby. It was closed for the season, except to run the rented condos and provide internet access for patrons. Bob Ritzau, the athletic director at Poly, had emailed, wondering if I remembered a former track athlete, Keith Neal. He had just recently passed away and his mother wished to include in the ceremony some of his track accomplishments. Could I help her remember them? Although half a world away, I was instantly back in Riverside, 1985, coaching a young man I had watched grow in confidence. I certainly remembered Keith. Although he must have been about 42 when he died, I remember his 18-year-old face and the promise of things to come. He ran on several of our championship relays, and anchored the 4 X 400 relay. One of his splits easily broke the school record, but couldn't count because he had a running start. No one in our league could come close to him. He had the fastest mile relay split of any Poly runner, ever—which is saying quite a bit! Yes, I remembered Keith Neal.

See epilogue chapter 19

DISCUSSION/REFLECTION QUESTIONS

CHAPTER 19   IRELAND

0. Who is the Prime Minister of Finland? (Just kidding.) Are
    you good at remembering things? What are you most likely
    to remember: Good things that happened to you or bad
    things?

1. Think of a time you received sad news while having a good
    time. Can you still remember being up, then being down,
    and the transition between? Do you think you might spend
    more time being down than others? If yes, what can you do
    to help yourself?

2. Read Deuteronomy chapter 8. Why is remembering so
    important?

3. When you are in a crisis, are you more likely to panic and
    forget how God has provided for you in the past, or to be
    confident remembering how God has helped you in the past?

4. How have you experienced God supporting you in the past
    year? What can you do to keep remembering how God is
    present with you?

CHAPTER 20   SMALL WORLD

(RE: March 2009)

We were told not to wear green or blue so as not to look like either a correctional officer or an inmate, and we were instructed not to give the inmates anything. As is the case in level one yards (lowest security), this level four yard (highest security) housed hundreds of men in a small area.

We arrived on Thursday, the first day of a four-day Kairos weekend at R. J. Donovan Prison. The first inmate I met was Quinn, a personable and open man. I soon learned that he followed Christ--and was praying his cellie would, too. A little later I found Danny, the one I would host. He was well-spoken and could easily and readily quote Scripture. When he asked what I did on the outside, I told him I was a retired math teacher. His face took on a look of astonishment. He then told me he was going for his GED, but needed to boost his math score. I told him I could help, if we could find some time.

Soon we chose our seats; I sat in the back--to be far from the booming sound system (twelve yards away.) Ansel and Arturo, two easy-going Native Americans, sat with me.

After a brief welcome, we each introduced ourselves. Several inmates stood out. Ben, arms folded, looked tough, then said he had come for the cookies; his eyes were somehow different than everyone else's. Rupert wore a special vest, which read "sight and hearing impaired." He had a patch over one eye. Jamison spoke so softly I could only make out some of what he said.

Afterwards Jim, the leader of this particular Kairos, brought in the "inside" team--fourteen inmates who had already been through a Kairos weekend and had returned to help and serve. As they came in and were lining up in the front of us, Arturo, sitting with Ansel and me in the back, stood and shouted with conviction, "That's him, number two!" Laughter resonated.

Jim offered a few more words of encouragement, then we broke into our groups. We were the family of Paul, comprised of six candidates, plus three of us from the outside. Was it a coincidence that we sat directly in front of the right speaker with Rupert and his vest on my left and Ben and his folded arms on my right? Joining us were Sergio, Kent, Jamison, and Ansel. Joining me from the "outside," Bruce served as the table leader and Mel as a pastor. We listened to speeches, ate cookies, discussed many things, made posters, prayed and ate more cookies. The group impressed and encouraged me. Rupert, Kent and Sergio were either strong Christians or working on it. Ansel was open and articulate and said he wanted to learn more. Ben did not even sing at first, but eventually opened up. He was the opposite of pretentious and was willing to discuss any topic in a completely straightforward manner.

The next day during a break Fr. Eric and I were listening to Danny. He said his father was a barber and that he himself had been cutting hair since he was twelve. Now he cut hair on the inside and spread the gospel while he worked. At lunch I helped him with some algebra. He did well.

Back in our groups, while listening to a talk, Ben began to slowly unravel his prison-issued t-shirt. When the strand became about a meter in length he gave me the end. At first I thought he was playing a joke on me. Then I thought he might get in trouble (even though no officers stayed in the "chapel" with us.) So I gave the end back to him and whispered, "The whole shirt is going to come undone." He said it would be okay and gave the middle of his growing strand to Gerrit who sat at another table but was only inches away when we faced the podium. Gerrit knew exactly what to do with it and promptly looped it over a finger. Ben used his teeth to cut the thin strand and began twisting the two free ends while he, Gerrit, and I listened. When he finished twisting, Ben tied the intertwined strand to his mug handle so he could tell his from the other Kairos mugs given to each candidate. During the next break, Ben offered that when you are in your house (cell), you can use a bar of soap to quickly twist strands into string and then cords; and that when you are in the hole (solitary confinement with zero accoutrements, zero apparel) if you are lucky enough to get some underwear you could remove the zigzag stitching and fashion a cord and attach a button, or small procured object, or bug, and go fishing. Fishing, he further explained, was for casting out onto the corridor's floor in hopes of hooking up with another inmate and using this connection to exchange whatever they could. I asked if they were allowed to have books in the hole and he said they were, so I imagine blank pages could be removed and then used as paper for writing (fingernails could make indentions to form letters, if nothing else).

Later that day Bruce, our family (table) leader, asked what we had learned from the weekend so far. Ben's answer was unexpected. He said he was amazed that we, the outside team, "could be anywhere you wished and you chose to spend it in prison with us. There is love here and I believe it is not an act, but real. No matter what happens I will remember this!"

Saturday morning started well, but Ben and Ansel did not show up. Once a participant drops out, rules say they can't come back. (This was an effort to stop inmates from coming and going.) Ben finally came, explaining that he had been delayed. Later I learned that Ansel did not come because he was afraid he would have to give up his Native American identity if he became a Christian.

Ben had told me he, Ben, used to be a big time racist, but had slowly abandoned his old ways. Now here we were, the family of Paul, sitting in a back room holding hands in prayer. Ben happens to be white and Jamison happens to be black and those two happened to be holding hands in our circle of brothers.

The outside team had written a letter to each and every candidate. These letters were assembled into personal bags and then letters were added from others who had taken the time to write to prisoners. These were called Agape, short for Agape letters. The outside team and the inside (helper) team waited outside the chapel so the candidates could read their Agape. Only they, a lone, soulful guitar player, the pastors, and a few others stayed. While waiting outside, I spoke with Stan from the inside team. He remembered when he received his Agape six months earlier. He described how hard the letters had hit him. He saved them all. He still pores over and over them. He wept as he recounted the content of some of the letters. He knew exactly what the men were going through on the other side of the wall on which we leaned.

A few minutes later, I was speaking with tall Rick, who was also on the inside team. He told me when he got his Agape six months earlier he "cried like a baby." He had not cried in many years and that now he didn't care who saw him cry. He was a good friend with Ben; they had both been part of the same group of Odinists. (Odinists value and esteem everything that sustains or enriches life and do not see life on Earth as being a preparation for a life hereafter.) He told me he has been praying for Ben. Later Rick shared that when he was on the run he stabbed a man with the street name Boxboy. Then in prison, years later, he stuck Boxboy again. But, Rick said, he was a different man now. I believed him, standing out in the sun in yard three, me in my long pants and Rick in his prison pants, prison shirt, and Kairos apron.

When we went back inside, silence charged the atmosphere. Some men were crying. Others purposely ignored their mail as they did not wish to be seen crying, since many prisoners view crying as a sign of weakness. Ben was misty-eyed, but quickly used his male anti-tearing skills to clean up. (Later Fr. Eric told me Ben would read a letter, be taken aback by how it hit him full on, then wait a few minutes to collect himself so he could attempt to read another without showing anyone what it was doing to him.) Ben rose as I walked over. A red-eyed Gerrit repeatedly said to Ben and me, "I am real emotional right now. I'm real emotional right now." To which Ben responded, "These (Kairos) guys really know what they are doing."

An opportunity to share with the entire group was given, and one of those who took advantage of that was Arturo. He had been deeply moved by a letter placed randomly in his bag written by a Granny Myrna. She spoke of the earth and what it takes to grow. It was precisely, astoundingly what the Native American needed to hear! Although Donovan is located on flat land with nearby hills, this weekend had become a mountaintop experience in one way or another for all with ears and eyes.

Jamison also used the open mike. Of course I could not understand all that he said, but he believed Christ as his Savior! Later he asked us to pray for his brother to join him. His brother was also in yard three, a fellow inmate.

By Sunday, most had had a chance to finish reading their hundred pieces (plus or minus a few) of Agape. At least, however, one did not want to read them.

We had a special lunch brought in for the candidates. Fajitas! When we got back to the chapel, the tables had been cleared out and about four dozen additional visitors were seated facing our empty chairs. We then sat in rows in our "families" facing them. After a few songs and speeches, candidates again stood at the open microphone. I was about to type, "Unbelievable!" to describe what came next, but that would have been wrong. They spoke entirely believable, unscripted, strong words from broken souls that had reached a state far from God, and now believed even they could be forgiven. (A few had told us in private that during the prison riots at Pelican Bay they had done "unspeakable things.") But here they were trying to explain this weekend to some who had been there the whole time, and some who were strangers.

Yancy, a candidate, said over the past several months he had been getting his hair cut by Danny. Yancy said Danny kept talking about the love of God and, "I wanted to run but I had that stupid sheet around me so I had to stay and listen." Stan, a man of few words, took to the mike and admitted, "I'm sweating so much, I'm more nervous than a snitch at a gangster party." Jamison went up, I can't remember what he said, maybe because I couldn't hear, but it was great on two counts: he was talking in public and his topic was the start of his new life in Christ!

We all knew the weekend had to end. As I said goodbye to each in the family of Paul, I asked if they would be back next Saturday. All said they would, with the exception of Ben. He said he probably wouldn't. I told him I was glad to have met him and appreciated his openness and willingness to listen and share. He really was insightful and honest.

One week later I spoke again with tall Rick. He got a new roommate. When he walked in, he recognized him: Boxboy (the man he had stabbed, twice)! Rick froze at the door for almost a minute. Finally he went in with his hands out to the side and palms open and said, "I am a changed man! Do what you gotta do." Boxboy did nothing. Rick slowly explained that he had accepted Christ as his Savior and that he had been forgiven and had forgiven those who had wronged him! He further explained, "You have nothing to worry about; I really am a changed man."

In the morning, Boxboy looked awful. He had not slept, certain that Rick would stick him again. Rick did his best to reassure him. The next morning Boxboy was in bad shape, having had no sleep for two nights, all the while thinking he was going to be knifed again. The next night Boxboy finally gave in and slept. Now, they are more than roommates; they are cellies. Something tells me Boxboy might be at the next Kairos. I guess not forgiving is akin to holding a burning coal and waiting for the other guy to say, "Ouch!"

Ben came after all. I had prayed for him, but didn't really expect to see him. What does that say about me? He believes all that he has seen is real and he has seen the major change in his friend Rick.

Soft-spoken Jamison said his mortal enemy from the streets was in yard three. Jamison said when they see each other, their entire focus is on the other. Unspoken contempt. Jamison said he told him he had forgiven him and asked for his forgiveness, but that no matter what, Jamison had forgiven him. It's a beautiful thing. Then he began thanking his cellie, Quinn, the first inmate I had met that first night and the one praying his cellie would become a Christian. Small world.

The names were changed, but not to protect the innocent. None of us were.

DISCUSSION/REFLECTION QUESTIONS

CHAPTER 20   SMALL WORLD

0. Try to imagine being stabbed. Try to imagine being locked in a small room with the big man who had stabbed you. Now imagine he tells you he is a Christian and that you have nothing to worry about. If you were a Christian, you could pray with him right then and there. Wouldn't that be great? What do you think others might do?

1. Who do you know personally that you would consider the least likely candidate to surrender to Christ?

2. Read Acts 9:1-22. Do you think such a radical life change is possible for the person you identified from question one? Why?

3. Read Matthew 9:36-38. This is a picture of what Jesus sees when he looks at people. What do you see when you look at others? Are you able to look at them through the eyes of Christ? Pray for that ability.

4. Read Luke 15:1-7. How does this passage speak to you? What in this passage motivates you? What challenges you? What will you do about it?

4. Read Luke 15:1-7. How does this passage speak to you? What in this passage motivates you? What challenges you? What will you do about it?

CHAPTER 21   AXE ACTS

(RE: April 2009)

Back in October of 1988, my wife, daughter, and I pulled up
stakes and moved to a little town in San Diego County called
Fallbrook. We purchased a few flats of seedling eucalyptus. I
asked some coworkers if they wanted some and Mike Neece took
advantage of a good deal. (Mike was the first person I heard who
used the quote, "Beware your thoughts; they become your words.
Beware your words; they become your actions. Beware your
actions; they become your habits.") I planted several dozen, to
be used someday as firewood. Possibly an ignoble end for a tree,
but I was planning ahead. (In most of the world dirt is free and
firewood isn't. I have since discovered the opposite in Fallbrook.
Who would have thought?)

My father was a dairyman. He got up early to milk the cows. He
processed milk, bottled milk, and took care of the cows and
business during the day. Every evening he milked the cows
again. He did this every single day of the year, without
exception. No weekends off, no sick days off, no holidays off, no
vacations. Just work. Thus, my father did not get to see many of
his children's extra-curricular activities.

In Little League I was the starting first baseman for the third
place Bloomington Tigers. He made special arrangements to
come see me play once. I started every game that year, except
two. The night he came, I did not play.

In High School I went out for basketball my senior year; I made
the varsity team. My main job was to guard a starter on our team
during practice. No one wanted to guard him, as he liked to push
all rules to the extreme. My father never came to a game, but I
didn't mind; I did not get much game time anyway. Regardless, I
used to play basketball all the time. In college I would play
whenever possible. In those days, if the waves were decent at
Laguna Beach or Newport, I would body surf. Otherwise I would
play pickup games on the courts in the sun. I discovered a truth
about myself. It did not matter what the other team thought of

me. It did not matter what my team thought of me. It only mattered what I thought my team thought of me! (Strange, but true.) The word confidence comes to mind.

While I was still in college, our church entered a basketball team in the community men's league. I was an average player on an average team, but I enjoyed the fun and exercise. Then my father announced he was going to come watch me play. Wow! I was nineteen and he was going to watch me play! My dad would be in the stands, watching! Wow!

Although I had not reached my full height, many times I was asked to play center. I wasn't very tall for a center, but I was the tallest starter we had. My father was there for tip-off. I surprised myself by out-jumping my opponent and tapping it straight to our point guard, Jess Swick. We set up our offense. I went in for an offensive rebound, but tipped it in instead. Play was fast. We traded missed shots, and I found myself as the deepest defender on their fast break. I matched stride for stride with their ball handler, who decided not to pass and went in for a lay-up.

Unbelievably, I did something I have never done before or since. High above the rim I pinned the ball to the backboard. We got the rebound and the shooter shouted to the ref, "That's goal tending." (Secretly I wanted him to call it. Me, goaltending! I'll tell my grandkids about it someday.) Back on offense we were having trouble getting anyone open, so I decided to take a baseline jumper. The man guarding me was a little shorter, but could jump higher than I could, so my jumper became a fall away jumper. Swish, even though I was fouled and knocked to the ground. After the free throw the score was five to nothing. I had won the tip off, blocked a shot, and scored all of our points and that was just the first minute! My father was there, and I knew he thought I was pretty good at math, body surfing, and basketball. I will not forget that night.

After the game my dad and I walked to the car. I know that probably doesn't sound like a big deal to you, but it only happened once, and has no chance of ever happening again. He knew plenty about life, but not too much about basketball. He commented on our win. He had no idea I had just played the game of my life. I was his son and played as he imagined his son would play, and that was enough.

A few weeks ago, Greg Coppock, a good friend from church, called and asked if I would play "the cross-maker" in "The Way of the Cross" at our church on Good Friday. Another good friend, Brad Britton, would be unable to do it on that particular day. Then Brad was asked to sing and suddenly I became the cross-maker for all three days.

Greg had asked me to write a script, but Jerome, the pastor of our church, thought the cross-maker should simply make a cross as people went from station to station in a private, contemplative manner. Later Jerome suggested that maybe the cross-maker should mention he was friends with Joseph and that a very young Jesus used to play in the shop. I wrote a short script and a little extra in case the pilgrims stayed longer to watch. Jerome liked it.

Usually when asked to write a sketch or children's sermon, I rehearse it a few times, perform it during first service, then maybe once again for second service. But this time I spoke while making a cross for big groups, small groups, and solitary travelers. The staging I had made up started with me sitting motionless on a large log with an axe on my knees. I had my head down and eyes closed. At an appropriate time I would come to life, a cross-maker making one more cross.

As I would sit on the log waiting to perform the drama, I would think through what I would say and do. Then, of course, when someone entered the large room, now a centuries-old wood shop, I would say and do what I had been mentally rehearsing. Somewhere around the sixth or tenth time this played out, I would no longer need to think through what was about to happen. So while waiting, I would pray for those who were about to come from witnessing the trial of Jesus of Nazareth into a room where they could listen and watch an old man in the process of fashioning a cross.

Somewhere around the twentieth time, I realized the experience was becoming more realistic ... to me! I had thought it. I had said it. I had acted it, over and over and over. As if I actually were a cross-maker saying things with the tonal inflections of a reminiscing voice I didn't know I had: "I knew his father, Joseph. Good carpenter. Good friend. Jesus was little back then. He would draw in the sawdust on the floor... He could stack wood chips higher than any of my sons ever could." And then I would stop the whet-stone-and-spit sharpening of my axe and say, "I don't recall that He ever played much with the nails though." I would then turn to look at a small pile of large spikes on the floor, before I would slowly continue sharpening the old tool balanced on my knees. I would get chills every time I said it.

Now I don't know if you, the reader, believe Jesus was the Son of God, or the opposite-- that He was just a man. Either way, I think we can agree that even if you ignore the Bible, the myriad of secular historians for the first several centuries wrote that Jesus lived and was crucified. Those events actually and most assuredly happened! He died believing, knowing, that He was giving his life for ours! There was a cross and Jesus was nailed to it.

As the scene continued, I would chop a mortise in a crossbar as I raged against Barabbas and an unseen crowd. I had a crossbar on which I could take out my anger, but the pilgrims could only watch. With each dramatization, the floor became more cluttered with wood chips and the sobs of several solo onlookers became more searing to my heart.

Here I was--a barefoot, bearded (well, two weeks growth), robe-wearing, axe-wielding man of the 21st century, growing with each depiction into the habits of the lone, first- century carpenter who made the cross used to crucify Jesus. With full arcs of the axe, the cross-maker would say, "Crucifixion (Strike), a terrible way to die! (Strike.) I've heard their moans. (Strike.) I've felt their screams. (Strike.) Those guards may not know much (Strike), but they know death. (Strike.) No one comes off a Roman cross alive (Strike). No one (Strike)! No one ever has (Strike)! No one ever will (Strike)! If all I had to do to avoid being crucified (Strike) was say, 'I'm not the son of God' (Strike), I'd say it a thousand times! (Strike.) I'm not the Son of God (Strike)! I'm not the Son of God (Strike)! Why didn't He say it? (Strike.) WHY DIDN'T YOU SAY IT? (Strike.)"

These particular eucalyptus trees did not meet the ignoble end I had imagined when I planted them. Instead, as the cross-maker chopped them, they acted as a reminder of the day the world changed; while I got to play for my father...one more time.

DISCUSSION/REFLECTION QUESTIONS

CHAPTER 21   AXE ACTS

0.   "Beware your thoughts; they become your words. Beware
     your words; they become your actions. Beware your actions;
     they become your habits." Do you think this is true? If yes,
     what can you do to guard your thoughts?

1.   In what ways did you try to rise to your dad's expectations?
     Why did you want to rise to his expectations or why not?
     Read John 12:27-28 and John 17:4-5. What does Jesus say is
     His desire and purpose?

2.   Read Romans 5:6-8 and 1 John 3:1? How has God proven
     His love for us? What amazes you about what these verses
     have to say?

3.   When you feel loved by someone, how do you respond to him
     or her? Read John 15:10, 1 Corinthians 10:31 and Colossians
     3:22-24. How are you to respond to God's love for you?

4.   Are you motivated to follow Christ out of love or out of a
     sense of obligation or fear? Does the motivation make a
     difference? Explain. What can you do to become more aware
     of God's love for you?

CHAPTER 22   BOY MEETS GIRL

(RE: 1971)

Sometimes I say, "The glass is half empty." Sometimes I say, "The glass is half full." Sometimes I say, "The glass is completely full: half liquid, half air." Sometimes, I say, "Hey, look, there's a spot on the glass." These are the pessimist, the optimist, the Christian, and the world in me.

In March of 1971, I pulled the car into the driveway of a ranch house near the corner of Archibald and Baseline in Cucamonga, California. I exited the only new car I would ever own, a 1970 Plymouth Roadrunner (Dukes of Hazzard), on the only blind date to which I would ever agree. (Thanks to Jess S. and Robin B.) I knocked on the door, not knowing my life would never be the same. "Hi, I'm Jerry."

A few hours later, after watching the re-release of "Gone with the Wind," we spoke of George Reeves (TV's original Superman-- who was in the movie's opening scenes), college, the war in Vietnam, and horses.

On our second date we went bowling, even though neither of us really liked bowling much. It was just the thing to do. Eventually we went to the beach. Later she watched me play a few basketball games and I watched her ride in a few classes at some horse shows. She watched me play a few games of men's fast pitch softball. I watched her ride in a few more classes at a few more horse shows.

I don't remember if we won or lost those particular basketball and softball games. I do remember how she did in each and every one of her classes at the various horse shows. She won. If participating in a small class, she won. If it was a huge class, she won. Whether she competed in English, or Western, or cart, or combination, or pleasure, or equitation, or amateur, or pro-am (she always kept her amateur standing), or trail, or costume, or command, she won! So I saw how she, her parents, and her horse, Star View's Cassiopeia, acted when they won. Adele would affectionately pat the horse, which they raised from a baby and trained into a champion themselves, on the neck. While continuing with her ever present smile she would hand the winnings to her mother on the way back to the stable and then Adele and her father would begin taking care of the horse and tack joined shortly thereafter by her mother. There was work to be done, and each knew exactly what to do. But it wasn't work. It was what this family loved, and I think "Classy" loved too.

As exciting as it was, somewhere after watching her fifteenth or thirtieth win, I secretly wished to see how Adele would act when she did *not* bring back the blue ribbon. Would she throw a tantrum, cry on her father's shoulder, blame the judge, kick the horse, become morose, or possibly even truculent?

Horse shows usually last somewhere between several hours and a week or two, and since I was still in college, I only got to see some of the classes she was in. It did not happen often, but sometimes she wasn't picked first by the judges.   But I had only heard about it, I wanted to see. For some reason I had it in my head that this was going to help me measure her character. I mean, after all, anyone can look great when they are repeatedly deemed the best, can't they?

It was late afternoon and the announcer called the ribbon winners of the huge class in reverse order, "Sixth place goes to... Fifth place to... Four place... Third... The second place award goes to number 131, Star View's Cassiopeia, Adele Reichers up, Bob Reichers owner..." This was it. Adele affectionately tapped "Classy" on the neck. While continuing with her ever present smile she handed the winnings to her mother on the way back to the stable and then Adele and her father began taking care of the horse and tack joined shortly thereafter by her mother. There was work to be done, and each knew exactly what to do. But it wasn't work.

I had never been to a horse show before I met Adele. But since we met, I've seen Adele guide a horse to do things that actually caused hair on the back of my neck to stand. My favorite class to watch was the Command Class—like "Simon Says" on horseback. In this class, the judge's opinion did not matter; everyone could spot mistakes or could see who was the last one to follow the command. Not every show offered command class, but when scheduled, it usually got the most entries.

Imagine thirty or more horses in a ring. The judge stands near the center and notifies the announcer through an assistant (often the Ring Master) what the horse and riders should do next. When a mistake was made, the horse and rider are dismissed from the ring. One by one they leave. When numbers get down to the last ten (or six, etc., depending on the number of awards to be given), those who would then misstep were to go to the ring's center to await the presentation of awards.

I remember one especially memorable show. Up to this point, Adele had been in 14 command classes in her life and all 14 had been firsts! When this competition got down to four horses, no remaining riders were making any mistakes. So to narrow the field further, the judge began to ask the riders to purposefully make the horse do something normally considered incorrect. When a horse canters, one leg naturally comes forward before the other. If he is curving, the horse's outside leg goes first, or leads (very logical, since that leg must travel farther). After the judge had the participants canter on the wrong lead, three remained. He then asked them to reverse direction...then to stop...then to go straight into a canter from a stop on the wrong lead. Now two remained. For the next four minutes Adele and her last competitor both executed whatever the judge could think of. The crowd cheered, clapped, and hollered. No one could remember anything like this, ever.

Finally, the judge asked them to stop, and pulling a rule from an equitation class (judged on the rider), had the riders dismount and switch horses. The win, of course, would now depend solely on the rider. After a few more minutes, the judge asked for the wrong lead. Only Adele perfectly executed the move—and won her 15th consecutive command class. She would be in nine more before she would retire; she won those too.

The opposite of this class was the costume class. If it took place at all, it was usually scheduled near the end of a rather large show. Adele called it a "fun class." Horses and riders would dress up and be judged, in part, on how coordinated their appearance was. Adele had a costume that looked like what Barbara Eden wore in "I dream of Jeannie." Adele did not need help getting off a horse, but with this lightweight arabesque ensemble, she did. You will just have to imagine how she looked riding the only black Morgan in the show in her sheer outfit at night. When I helped her down, I was shocked that my fingers were only a half-inch short of going all the way around her waist.

In October 1973, during an ongoing rivalry between the two coasts as to which had the best horses, the first Morgan Nationals were held. Cassiopeia won three of her classes and at the concluding banquet a shy girl from Cucamonga was seated next to Mrs. Levi-Strauss and directly across from Mrs. Archibald Cox (the wife of the Watergate Prosecutor.) Her horse won more blues at the Nationals than any other, so headquarters sent a photographer from New York out here for a picture. It came out so well the picture was used on a magazine cover and then giant blow-ups of it were hung all over the nationals the following season. The Morgan Horse Magazine used it as a type of logo for many years. It's a great picture, but if you look closely, you can see that Adele's cheeks are swollen from having all her wisdom teeth extracted the day before. She did not throw a tantrum, cry, blame anyone, or become morose or even truculent.

Adele retired from showing horses in 1987, but continues as a show steward (the answer-woman who knows all the rules). Don't tell anyone, but she would steward horse shows for free. She does cash the checks they send her, however.

So, am I lucky or blessed?

I did not know how to end this story, but now I do. Secondly with a note I sent to the women in my life and firstly with a highly altered semi-famous quote:

I gave Adele some groceries and she gave me a meal.

I gave Adele a house and she gave me a home.

I gave Adele nine months and she gave me a daughter.

Now her mother is telling me to never give her a piece of my mind.

Dear Adele and Laura,   Mother's Day 2006,

At the conclusion of first service today, I was sitting up front with my left arm out on the pew top, listening to the organist play the postlude, while fifteen to twenty of us stayed to hear the beautiful music (my usual practice.)

After a minute or so, retired marine Colonel Rufus Bowers came up and sat on my immediate left. He asked about my wife and daughter and I informed him Adele was in Palo Alto at a horse show and Laura had just graduated from college. (I didn't mention that Laura had just become engaged.) He said he remembered when I used to give children's sermons and that a couple weeks ago he was mowing the lawn (in Tennessee) and recalled one such sermonette where I picked up Laura.

Then he paused. I finally told him that I remembered those messages, but that I didn't remember that one. (I was thinking maybe he mistakenly thought the little girl I picked up for the story "Swinging in the Reign" was my daughter.) He finally got out that he thought I had said it was going to be the last time I would pick up Laura, as she was getting too big to do so. Suddenly I remembered picking her up. I remembered it was at the conclusion of the children's sermon, I remembered the dress Laura was wearing, I remembered turning our backs to the congregation to look at the stained glass window of Jesus and his outstretched arms, I remembered Laura's hair and head against my right cheek. (I later remembered that the children's sermon told about being in God's loving arms and how good it was to have a Father who could "pick you up" at any time. And I remembered that I had just been cleared to pick up Laura after recuperating from surgery.)

Rufus took off his glasses because he was crying. He tried to say more, but could not. I had my arm around Rufus, as I remembered my little girl, how I used to pick her up and set her on my hip. A time gone by. Rufus and I sat there together, that Sunday morning, with the organ playing and our tears falling from memories past.

After several more stanzas, Rufus composed himself enough to finish telling me what he had come over to say. I couldn't tell you what he said, and it doesn't matter. I imagine those who stayed wondered what was going on, but somehow knew not to interrupt. I imagine the marine and I weren't thinking identical thoughts, the thoughts a father has.

Laura, thank you for making us proud, time after time.

Adele, thank you for marrying me, making me a father, and causing so many wonderful memories.

 Happy Mother's Day,

Jerry

See epilogue chapter 22.

DISCUSSION/REFLECTION QUESTIONS

CHAPTER 22   BOY MEETS GIRL

0. Can you pinpoint a time in your life when things would change and get even better? Can you still recall details of the event?

1. Read Psalm 128. What is the promise? What is required?

2. What do you think it means to "fear the Lord"? How would we show this kind of fear? Share practical ways that this kind of fear would bring blessings to a marriage and family.

3. Read Psalm 107. What is each group of people encouraged to do? Why?

4. How have you experienced God's blessing in small and big ways today, this week, this month, this year? Whom have you told?

CHAPTER 23 BEN

(RE: Sept. 2009)

Our friends the Brittons had one dog too many. We helped them out. Not many wanted him, maybe because he had one flop ear and the other dogs wouldn't let him play in any reindeer games. But he is just lovable. He was famous for fetching, but not bringing, whatever it was, back. I was determined to fix that. At first he would get into trouble often, but I later found it was due to the fact that I did not speak dog.   His name was Benny, but now that he is two, we call him Ben. I think Ben thinks I can do no wrong. He reminds me of that prayer: "Lord help me to be half the man my dog thinks I am."

Ben doesn't care how I dress, how I look, or how old I am. And speaking of age, I recently turned six decades and you only do that once. Usually Adele and I simply go out for dinner to celebrate both our birthdays; they are only three days apart. Several years ago we spoke of having a party for some "milestone" birthday or maybe even a surprise party, but that would be work, and besides, it is so peaceful out here all alone in the country. When I asked Adele if she would want me to surprise her, she made it clear she would much rather just go out to dinner and not be "put on the spot" at a surprise party and to "Please, never throw me a surprise party." Well, this year we went out to dinner at a fun restaurant in San Diego; we had heard good reports about it. Not sure if we were commemorating Adele's birthday or our birthdays. Either way, the evening was rather nice.

Several weeks earlier I had received a suspicious email on an old address Adele and I used to share. She explained it away, but I thought maybe it held clues to a surprise party. You see, my sixtieth birthday happened to fall on a Sunday, a day just perfect for an afternoon surprise party. Perfect!

(Special Note: There is a sound some men make when their hard work is destroyed in a split second or when something doesn't go the way they had planned or imagined. They open their mouth, lips stationary, and they force air over their tightened larynx causing a sound about three octaves higher than their normal speaking voice, followed by a slightly lower tone, ending with a tone matching the first, and all kind of slurred together. It sounds like a sympathetic whine and lasts about seven tenths of a second. (But I am getting ahead of myself. More on this later.)

Two friends of mine, Tom, Dale, and I had scheduled to prepare the ground east of my garage for a three-way mutual garden. We planned to do this after church...church is on Sunday...Sunday was my sixtieth birthday! Everything was coming together; would I be able to convincingly act surprised?

One of the tasks I was supposed to do before the Sunday workday was to get some dirt to level the proposed area. With the help of my tractor "Diesel" and my faithful dog, this would be short work. Diesel, a Kubota, is orange, while Ben, a German shepherd, is tan and black. Ben goes wherever I (and Diesel) go. There is a spot, about a hundred yards down the driveway where I have been securing dirt lately. When I get a scoop in the Kubota, Ben always comes too. He actually waits until I have a full bucket before he finds the largest possible dirt clod to carry up. He carries it in his mouth. Sometimes it falls apart before he gets there but he usually makes it to the top. Quite a sight.

Ben also collects firewood. He has a firewood collection. He can carry gigantic pieces in his mouth. The pieces larger in diameter than his jaws were meant to open he picks up by sinking his bottom canines (no pun intended) into the smooth flat circular end and his top canines into the cylindrical side. The mass usually hangs off to his left, so the weight causes his head to swivel about sixty-five degrees counter-clockwise as he prances to his goal. He debarks (no pun intended) the chunks and eats portions of the wood. I used to worry about splinters, but he appears to be impervious to slivers of wood.

Another of his favorite things is to retrieve fallen oranges and then drop them at my feet--in hopes I will toss them, so he can fetch. (He also does this with firewood and avocados. I taught him to do that. Specifically, I taught him to go get rollie things and place them at my feet. Is it a good idea to place rollie things at the feet of a sexagenarian?) He then eats the orange. Now that he has consumed all of the hundreds of fallen oranges, he picks fresh oranges off the trees.

Hornets like to buzz him and his oranges. He likes to snap at them. (It sounds like that last sound the "N-e-s-t-l-e-s Nestle's makes the very best chooooooooooocolate" dog made from the fifties.) I estimate he catches about one in twelve. (Bees are easier: 47%.) When he catches one, he spits it out so he can see it. Then he eats it. He's a good hunter, I guess. I thought that once a hornet stung him, he would stop snapping at them, but I thought incorrectly.

A few weeks ago I was preparing to mow the lawn. I had previously discovered that if I mow a strip and then move one of Ben's logs onto a mowed strip, he will move it back to the unmowed area. So, while Ben had one log in his mouth, I quickly tossed, two by two, his ten other logs over into the grove. Ben was taken aback by what he was seeing. It was then that he made that three-tone man-sound. The look on his face begged for empathy. He believed what he had seen and I believed what I had heard. Priceless.

Ben can help me get dirt, get firewood, pick oranges and kill hornets. Unfortunately, he has no way to help me paint the house, except when he lies on the tarp to keep it from blowing away. Ben is currently tan, black, and yellow. On hot days, Ben always finds a shady spot to watch me work. Should you have occasion to stop by you might affectionately say, "There's Ben and Jerry."

The morning of my sixtieth, Adele sang "Happy Birthday" to me (as she does every year). Then I opened her card and the other cards I had received. Then we went to church. Upon our return, I announced, "I'm going to put on my work clothes."

She said, "Okay, have fun doing man stuff." So, the surprise would be later! Dale and Tom had to be in on it; they had to know. They showed up wearing work clothes, not party clothes. Must be an evening party! Dale did some more tractor work while Tom and I dug the holes for the posts. (That's right. The holes were dug by...wait for it...wait for it...Tom and Jerry.)

I love logic. But things don't always happen logically. (Like the bumper sticker: If the world were logical, men would ride sidesaddle.) Logically, one would think nails should be placed perpendicular to the surface of the wood and then pounded in. But if you place them at an angle, you form a stronger bond, easier to hammer, and faster. Logically one might think the best way to extinguish a candle's flame via breath would be to cup the hand behind the tiny fire to coral the man-made wind and lessen the possible splattering of wax. But if a solitary finger is placed between the mouth and flame a few inches from the flame, a sharp exhale will extinguish the flame, yet not displace the melted wax.

The day wore on and I used more logic. Either Dale and Tom are really good actors, or there is no surprise party. Well, it was the latter. Although using logic, it is not excluded from the realm of possibilities that Dale and/or Tom might be really good actors.

Maybe I should tell Adele I would like a surprise party for my sixty-fifth (should I live that long), but then it wouldn't be a surprise, would it? That is why a teacher cannot announce he will give a pop (surprise) quiz the following week. Should he make such an announcement, he especially cannot then give the quiz on Friday. And Wednesday night a logical student would think, "The teacher can not give the pop quiz on Friday, so the quiz must be Thursday. But now that would not be a pop quiz." So Thursday is out too. And on Tuesday night....

Speaking of ladders, the next day I painted some more (exterior house walls, not ladders.) Tom, who recently had a hip replaced, helped me paint. He painted low and I painted high. He said his hip hurt less while painting than when he sat at the office. He told me that he liked the work and the company. Tom is nice. With the low stuff now completed, I needed to finish the high portions. When painting, one can get a lot of thinking in.

Somewhere around the third or fourth hour, I thought, Wouldn't it be funny if Sarah Palin married Ralph Nader, as her name would then be... well, I thought it was funny, but then I was a captive audience, Sarah Nader.

Wednesday my brother Jim and I (Huh. Jim and I: Gemini) flew to Sacramento, picked up another brother, Ralph, and the three of us flew to Washington where our older brother, Jack, picked us up. The following day we went on a great bike ride around the capitol. Now the way I worded it, you don't know if we flew in a private or commercial plane or jet or whether we flew to Washington State or D.C.

Got home late Friday. Early Saturday, I went to a Kairos prison ministry meeting with Art and Norm. On the way home I stopped to get the mail (a quarter mile from home) but about 20 seconds later while at the bottom of our driveway I saw balloons attached to the address pole I had made. I first thought that Adele must be having a shower. Then I thought, "But she would have told me." As I drove up I saw dozens of cars parked in the areas I had built for such a purpose with Diesel. I saw no people. Then Ben came running to me. He was so happy to see me and, Surprise! He was wearing a big blue birthday bow.

Jerry

DISCUSSION/REFLECTION QUESTIONS

CHAPTER 23   BEN

0. In the story, Ben always wanted to help: bring dirt up the driveway, move firewood, kill hornets, get oranges. Is there someone you would like to help? Take time right now to figure out a way to help.

1. Who are your best friends? What makes them your best friends?

2. Read Proverbs 17:17 and 18:24. Do you have friends that fit these descriptions? Do you fit this description?

3. Do you find it easy or hard to make close friends? Explain?

4. What can you do to strengthen a friendship this week? What can you do for or with a friend?

CHAPTER 24   BLINDED BY THE FACTS

(RE: 1955)

Two short stories: The first concerns a letter written almost two thousand years ago. A man named Peter wrote a letter in which he said, "... add to your faith goodness; and to goodness, knowledge; and to knowledge, self-control; and to self-control, perseverance; and to perseverance, godliness; and to godliness, brotherly kindness; and to brotherly kindness, love."

Later in this letter, he said that those who don't have these things are "nearsighted and blind." They don't see the gift that Jesus gave us: salvation. They were nearsighted and blind (yes, they) because they didn't recognize the Truth that was right in front of them.

The second story took place when I was five. My father had just sold his dairy in Paramount, and we were living in a tract home while he looked into buying another dairy. We lived there for a year, just two houses away from the Grant family. The Grants had a son just my age; his name was Chucky. He had a blind sister named Judy and she was three years older. My sister Dixie was born three years before me, so we played with the Grants a lot.

Judy asked her father if they could have a swimming pool. He said they couldn't afford it, but with a wheelbarrow and a shovel he dug an entire full-size backyard swimming pool. Not many people back then had swimming pools, but the Grants did, and we got to go over there and play. One sunny day I found myself in the pool with Judy, Chucky, and a lady I knew named Mrs. Crane. I can't remember where she lived, but she came and visited sometimes, and she had two children that were just a little younger than I. I went over to Mrs. Crane and asked her a question.

Before she could answer, Judy asked, "Why do you call your sister, Mrs. Crane?"

I responded, " Well, she's not my sister."

And Judy said, "Is so!"

I said, of course, "Is not!"

"Is so!"

"Is not!"

I knew I was going to win this debate, so I asked in a tone inviting agreement, "Mrs. Crane you aren't my sister, are you?"

She replied, "Of course I am. You know that."

I got out of the pool and ran home; my mother was standing at the kitchen sink.

I said, in my best five-year-old matter-of-fact voice, "Mom, Mrs. Crane isn't my sister, is she?"

She told me, "Of course she is! Now get out of here. You are dripping all over the floor."

That's when and how I found out Mrs. Crane was my sister, my sister Marilyn!

Now, before you jump to too many conclusions, let me defend myself. She was eighteen years older than I. She married when I was one; I don't remember the wedding. She had a different last name than the rest of our family. In fact, she had a family of her own. She didn't live in our house with the rest of my siblings and our parents; she had a house of her own. She came over and called my mom, "Mom", but my dad called my mom, "Mom," too. It was a term of endearment. Her husband called my mom, "Mom." but I didn't think he was my brother! She was in our family photo album, but so were our friends and neighbors. When looking through that book of pictures with me, I never heard anyone say, "That's your sister, Marilyn and that is your brother, Jack, and that is one of our neighbors Mr. Potts and that's ..." I just heard, "That's Marilyn, that's Jack, that is Mr. Potts, and that's ..." I knew many facts about Marilyn. But there was a truth I never heard, a reality I did not even imagine. I could see fully well, but I had been blind to the truth.

Judy Grant was physically blind. Although she couldn't see, she knew more than I did (especially on this topic.) And she is the one who told me Mrs. Marilyn Crane was my sister. I did not believer her, but I went to the source and found her a truth teller.

When Peter wrote that letter two thousand years ago, that's what he was talking about.

See epilogue chapter 24

DISCUSSION/REFLECTION QUESTIONS

CHAPTER 24   BLINDED BY THE FACTS

0. Can you remember a time when you were shocked by a fact?
    Come on, it must have happened several times; maybe not as
    dramatically as in Jerry's story, but it happened. You knew
    many details, but not this one. Sometimes the unknown
    details are more important than the known. Remember this
    the next time you are in the middle of a disagreement.

1. Have you ever had an experience where God has been
    working in and around your life, but it was not until later that
    you were able to look back and recognize the work of God?
    What happened?

2. Read 2 Peter 1:3-9. What catches your attention in this
    passage? What is eye-opening? What is the motivation for
    adding the qualities mentioned in this passage? What will be
    the result of doing so?

3. Why does Peter say that living a godly life is not only
    possible, but expected? Does this empower you or frighten
    you? Why?

4. Why does Peter say we are blind if we do not exhibit these
    qualities in our life? What are we blind to? What can you do
    to open your eyes?

CHAPTER 25   A TALE OF TWO MEN

(RE: Oct. 22 – 25, 2009)

In the first of four days at another Kairos "weekend" in Donovan State Prison we stood individually to introduce ourselves to the other 70 men. All stood except one inmate: Jimmy Lee. He said if he stands very long, he shakes, so he sat as he told us how he had believed he had no reason to live. In fact, he had attempted suicide six times. A Muslim for fourteen years, he sat directly in front of me; I could see the sleeves of his prison uniform shake.

When we split into pre-assigned groups of nine, Jimmy sat not at my table, but in an adjacent seat. We all sang Christian songs that I knew and for some reason, on the second day I watched Jimmy as we sang. He held the songbook with both hands, as though it were precious. He sang looking straight down at the book. He concentrated on the good news in the words, words telling a story he had not heard. At the song's conclusion, unlike everyone else, he continued to pore over the words. While the rest in the room were deciding what to sing next, Jimmy was studying. So was I, as I looked at him. This was real. This was the turning point. This was a man on the brink. It looked as if his eyes were welling, and I know mine were. I wondered if this might be too much for him to absorb in such a short time.

The biggest man in the room, Tom, sat at my table, "The Family of Luke." Tom said he was curious about the weekend and also had heard about the cookies. (Christian families had made hundreds of dozens of cookies for the prisoners. Homemade cookies aren't on the prison menus.) Tom had an open mind—and so he listened and shared.

The following day much happened. At open mike Jimmy Lee was one of those who wished to speak. I knew from previous conversations that he had been abused in foster homes from the age of three and since some of these foster parents were Christians (or at least claimed to be), he had not touched a Bible in decades. Furthermore, he had been in prison for over thirty years and felt he should be, because if he were out, he might kill someone. Jimmy told those in the room that he had never looked forward to any day in prison, but that day he did. He said he could not wait to get to Kairos. He said he wanted to live. He said the love he felt in the last three days was more than he had felt in all his previous years combined. Jimmy announced that he had never received a single letter while in prison, but as it turned out, that morning each candidate was given a bag with over 100 prayerfully written letters. Inmates do not receive sealed letters, but many of these were sealed because they were finalized in prison by the outside team (the Kairos volunteers). To Jimmy these were not letters, they were treasures. Unlike the other candidates, Jimmy would not open all his that day. Instead he would open one each day over a period of three months to savor the individual gifts.

Tom accepted Christ as his Lord and Savior that day! He told me he was excited to tell his wife and ten-year-old daughter all about it. His smile stretched joy across his face.

Later, Pastor Roger, who comes to the prison several times each week, performed "The Cross Ceremony". Each person is told, "Christ is counting on you!" If you respond, "I am counting on Christ." you are given a small wooden cross plus a big "thank you for coming" hug. In all other cases you are given a big "thank you for coming" hug. Tom and Jimmy both got hugs. Of the two, only Tom took a cross.

The next day was Sunday and was the last day. At the closing ceremony, with several outside visitors in attendance, each of the six tables/families went up to the mike, while one candidate gave a brief summary of some of the things the men in their family experienced before and during Kairos. The family of Luke picked Kip to report. Kip was a large, dyslexic, soft-spoken artist. From his painstakingly written notes he gave a superior accounting of the feelings of the candidates at our table. Back at our seats I took a piece of paper with our table name on it and added his full name in smaller print at the top. Then I wrote A+ and encircled it and had it passed all the way down our row to Kip. Later he enthusiastically notified me that, "I'm gonna keep this!" I wondered if it was his first "A" from a teacher.

When my friend Art mentioned we would have open mike again, Jimmy Lee spoke first. He wanted to explain why he had not accepted the cross the day before. He said that a growing percentage of Muslims believe they will be killed if they convert. Many of those are in prison. Jimmy Lee had been one such Muslim. But now he no longer wanted to be looking over his shoulder all the time. He wanted to live. He had hope. He loudly proclaimed that he is "counting on Christ and will take that cross now if you still have it." I jumped to my feet and shouted. I guess I should have felt pretty stupid, except for one thing. Everyone else did exactly that. Everyone. We knew the story. We knew he firmly believed there would now be men in the yard out to kill him. We watched him transform from a shaking mouse to an independent lion.

At the end, we men serenaded our visitors with what some call our anthem, "Abba Father." We sang so loudly that I actually sang several times louder than I normally talk, as no other human could possibly hear me. (I'm not tone deaf; I know I'm hitting wrong notes.) Then I went to Jimmy Lee. I remembered meeting a rather large, Yard Three former Muslim leader named Oscar at a previous Kairos reunion. Oscar, who had put his trust completely in Christ, was still alive and still lived in Yard Three. I told Jimmy Lee his life wouldn't be easy, but it would definitely be better.

The names were changed, but not to protect the innocent, none of us were.

DISCUSSION/REFLECTION QUESTIONS

CHAPTER 25   A TALE OF TWO MEN

0. In some countries, converting from Islam to Christianity is a capitol offense, as is the act of telling the Good News to a Muslim. Yet people explain and people accept everyday. Would the threat of death keep you from talking? What scares you?

1. Have you ever been in a situation where you were afraid to be recognized as a Christian? What was the reason?

2. Read Psalm 23. In what ways would this Psalm be good news to Jimmy Lee?

3. When we are confident that God is with us, what will we experience in our own life? How can you build confidence in God's presence? How did David build such confidence?

4. Feeling anxious, worried or afraid? Read the following passages out loud (believe it or not, it's more powerful when you hear it). Print them out and put them in places you'll see frequently. Memorize them and repeat them. Soon, the truth will sink in and your confidence will grow. Romans 8:31, 1 John 4:4, Psalm 27:1-3.

CHAPTER 26   CHOICES
(RE: 1956)

When we were little, others made many of our choices for us:
where to live, what to wear, when to eat. I don't know if this fact,
plus being the sixth of six siblings and the youngest kid in class
had anything to do with being shy. I do know that I devoted
much of my thinking to looking for ways to blend in.

One highly unusual day near the end of the school year at Alpha
Lyman, those of us in Mrs. Holland's first grade class had the
entire playground to ourselves. The boys were jumping over one
another out on the four-acre grass field, while the girls busied
themselves at the woodworking cart. One of the boys suddenly
shouted to the girls, "Watch this!" With all eyes on him, he
jumped over a boy who was down on all fours. I was six and
good at jumping, but few knew it. Shy, you may remember. But I
had seen it done. I was about to jump over Darrel Grapes who
was upright on his knees. I might not be able to get the attention
of all the girls, but I could get the attention of at least one. Yes,
one. I could do that. I do not know the origin of the temporary
spike in my courage, but I called out, "Hey, Betty, watch this!"

Well, Betty stopped sawing and looked over, as did all the girls.
They saw Darrel Grapes on his knees and me backing up to about
forty yards away, getting ready to run up and jump over him. I
had done it before; I would do it again. This would be easy;
jumping over Darrel was no problem. I had already finished the
hard part, saying to the cutest girl in the whole school, "Hey
Betty, watch this!" So I started running. Twenty yards later I was
going full speed. While running, I realized that my approach was
way too long, but no problem. I just kept running. Finally I took
off, high into the air, much higher than the top of the head of my
good friend Darrel Grapes. This was great! Things would be
different now. Once at the peak of my bold jump, I involuntarily
started my descent. If only Darrel had been a yard or two closer
to where I had taken off! Now that I had launched, I considered
my limited options. I pulled my feet up as best I could. I do not
remember hearing the stylish, pointy-toed shoe of my left foot hit
Darrel in his left temple. I do remember feeling the top half of

my body quickly passing the bottom half. By the time I got up, the whole class had encircled the temporarily unconscious clump on the grass we used to call Darrel.

"Who is it?"

"Darrel."

"What's wrong with him?"

"He's dead!"

"Who killed him?"

"Jerry."

Darrel finally started to move, then got up, and shortly thereafter announced he was okay. I was glad I had not killed him, but as everyone went back to what they were doing I wanted to say something like, "Wait, I really can do this. Darrel come back. My step was off...the wind..." But no, the opportunity had passed. I felt sorry I had hurt Darrel, as I, with my grass-stained knees, elbows, and face stood alone.

We grew up a little and became teens. We began to make more decisions, some of us to show our independence from our parents: What clothes to wear, how to wear them, who to hang with, how to behave. Some of us became two people, one at home and one at school. But if you think about it, we learned to make most of our choices by watching others.

Our Junior High principal, Mr. Perot Nevin, was into fitness. Back in the early sixties popular opinion said that athletes should not lift weights as one could become "muscle bound" and thus lose some range of motion. But our principal went against conventional wisdom and correctly urged several dozen high school athletes to come every Wednesday night to his back yard where he literally had tons of free weights. He also invited me, a shy twelve-year-old eighth grader. I did not really want to go, as I would be an eighth grader in with a bunch of high school students I didn't even know. But the principal had encouraged me, and I realized that it would probably be good for me.

I almost didn't go; I thought it over at length and finally managed to summon enough courage to show up. From that night on, I worked out every Wednesday night with a pack of senior high athletes. Sometimes they would tell stories. I remember listening to an athlete explain a little about wrestling to a handful of football players. He said your opponent is like a table; take away one of the four legs, push in that direction and it will fall over. Made sense to me. He then went on to describe a move called "The Wizard." He said that if you are in the "down" position, as directed by the referee, you are on all fours. Your opponent usually places his left hand on your left wrist and his right hand around your torso and on your stomach. He vividly described that on the command to wrestle, the down man could quickly move his right hand toward his own stomach and firmly grasp his opponent's right hand, thus securing one leg of the table, then immediately and vigorously roll toward his right shoulder causing the other wrestler to come along. He further described that a speedy spin, followed by a sweeping motion that lifted the other man's legs into the air, could cause a vertical orientation with the opponent's shoulders pinned under his own weight. That was pretty cool. They told other stories, too, but I remembered that one because of the name, "The Wizard," and because I could see it in my mind. I may have been shy, but I know how to listen to stories.

Once we become adults, we gain total control of our choices. Though you may question this fact, in reality we make choices based on past experience or belief and then develop patterns that may or may not be good for us. Some of our choices have long-term impacts. For example, when I graduated from college with a degree in mathematics, I thoughtfully narrowed my choices down to two: drive a Granny Goose Potato Chip truck for $13,000 a year or teach math for $8,000 a year.

We go through life making choices guided by our past. The choices of our past have enormous effect on our future. You or I can change the way we make choices if we wish. It is usually not hard, but it does take effort. We can see whether or not we are at the bottom of a rut. Each of us has the power to stop, look around, step out of that rut, look around again and walk away.

And if we find ourselves headed for that rut or actually somehow back in it, no one can stop us from stepping out again. We have the power to make choices.

Out of numerous virtues, one of the most respected is the ability to think independently. People with this gift, or honed skill, are not afraid to listen, not afraid to ask hard questions, and are courageous enough when making a decision to disallow what others might think. They understand that the right thing is not always the easy or popular thing. It is easy to be a follower and difficult to make one's own way. This path holds both risk and tremendous reward.

When something around us happens, we can either react or respond. A reaction is an emotional reflex. Have you ever said something and as soon as you said it wished you could take it back? (Yeah, me too.) That illustrates a reaction. Can you see how many of our choices in the past have been a reaction to the conditions at the moment? ("Hey Betty, watch this!") Taking time to think about the effect our choices will have can give us a new perspective.

On the other hand, a response is a considered action. (I almost didn't go; I thought it over at length and summoned enough courage to show up to the principal's backyard.) It takes a lot of practice to make an important and consistent change. I still have a long way to go.

At a middle school not far from my college, I accepted my first teaching job: a one-year position comprised of two eighth grade Algebra 1's and three seventh and eighth grade boys' PE classes. Things went all right in the PE classes, I suppose. We played football for several weeks, then basketball for a handful of weeks. In one class there was a natural leader with the nickname Quatch (Sasquatch, because he was so much bigger and taller than his peers.) He was 6'1", muscular, coordinated, personable, and a straight "A" student. Sometimes when I was demonstrating a drill or technique, I would use him as a partner.

We had no locker room. There were hooks numbered one through sixty on the inside perimeter of a normal-sized classroom. The students would come in, change into PE clothes, hang their street clothes on a hook, go out, exercise, come back in, wipe off using water from a combination drinking fountain and sink, dry off using paper towels, don their street clothes and depart. The rainy day plan was to take old mats and mattresses down from the rafters so that two boys at a time could wrestle one another while the other fifty-eight sat against the wall.

The first rainy day it worked like a charm. The two boys wrestling were always trying their best, and others cheered for them. Good thing it was fun, since it rained seventeen school days in a row that year. (Well, one of those days was sunny, but the fields and courts were flooded.) Somewhere around the tenth or twelfth day, morale started going downhill fast. The two wrestling were fine, but the other fifty-eight had cabin fever. One particular troublemaker convinced those along the wall to chant, "Maurer verses Quatch! Maurer verses Quatch!"

Please imagine yourself as a first year teacher with little experience charged with maintaining some sense of control over sixty young boys with extended cabin fever all in a 30 X 40 foot room. I had almost been doing that for two weeks. While officiating one particular match, I surmised that if I did wrestle Quatch and won, not much would change, but if I lost, I could lose whatever control I had left. I don't know if that reasoning was sound, but I knew I had absolutely nothing to gain and possibly much to lose. I was nine years older, two inches taller, and maybe a couple dozen pounds heavier than Quatch, but I did not know the most important stat. I did not know if he had more wrestling experience than my lifetime total of six or seven minutes.

When the current match concluded, I motioned for two more to take their places. Boos oozed out from the onlookers. Moments later our friend had the room chanting, "Maurer's a chicken. Maurer's a chicken." Now I reasoned that not wrestling would be worse than losing. I looked at my watch and hoped the current match would last another twenty minutes. Soon one of the wrestlers held his opponent's shoulder blades to the mat. "Pin!" I yelled. A cheer came from the onlookers. "Good effort." I said to the one who got up last. Maybe this would be a good time to give a long speech and point out how gracefully this young man just accepted defeat. On second thought, no.

"Quatch, get ready." A roar came from the onlookers. I handed my lanyard and whistle to the boy who would oversee the student/teacher match up. The boy was the one who had started the chanting. Since there was no room to start in the upright position, all contests commenced in the "down position." I went to all fours thinking that if I lost I would at least know I had given Quatch the advantage--or maybe that would be my excuse. I had won and lost literally hundreds of contests over the years, but somehow, this one seemed far more important than it should have. Why did I think so much rode on the outcome? I had made so many mistakes in that first year of teaching. I learned a lot.

I could hardly hear the sharply shouted command, "Wrestle!" over the exhortations bouncing off the walls. Although you probably weren't in that room, something tells me you not only know what I was going to try, but you also know the name of the move. I had heard it described almost a decade before when I was almost Quatch's age. The much-anticipated match lasted roughly five seconds.

"The Wizard" worked! I couldn't believe it! They couldn't believe it! A sudden silence hit. Inside I was screaming, "Yes!" Meanwhile, the students witnessed me pointing to two boys, while calmly saying, "You. You. On the mat." You may have heard those stories where some teacher rips a phone book in half or staples a tie to his chest (with an unseen body cast under his shirt) or some such thing and then had "no problems" the rest of the year. The awe-factor does not last long, but I must admit, I had no problems the rest of that day.

In order to make a significant change, we need to make better choices. Better choices come from responding rather than reacting. The phrase, "always think of others" might be good advice, but it does not mean at the exclusion of yourself! Some sociologists claim you will make approximately 225 non-trivial choices tomorrow. See if you can catch yourself reacting, then stop and make a better choice.

See Epilogue Chapter 26.

DISCUSSION/REFLECTION QUESTIONS

CHAPTER 26   CHOICES

0. Do you remember a time in your life you had to summon all your courage to do something? If you did it, how did you feel when it was over?

1. What choices did you make recently that were reactions? What choices did you make that were responses? What were the results? What do your reactions and responses reveal about the strength of your faith in God?

2. Read Hebrews 11:24-28. What choice did Moses make? Do you think this was a reaction or a response? Why?

3. On this matter we can use our hindsight. Moses could not. Why in the world would Moses make such a career-ending choice?

4. With this passage in mind, what criteria can you use to make wise, godly choices?

CHAPTER 27   ON TRACK TOO

(RE: 1947)

In 1947 a young boy threw a rock and it changed the world! Two years later the communists gained control over China. Some citizens correctly recognized that this event would mean an almost complete loss of freedom. They further noticed that public dissidents were rarely seen or heard from again, so they escaped to the island of Taiwan. A few months later, I was born. This is important to you, since if this had this not happened, you would not now be reading these words.

A decade later I awoke with an intense pain in my calf. In the morning I mentioned this to my mother, who identified it as a cramp and told me to rub it, if it happened again. This was good to know. When the pain recurred, I sadly discovered that massage didn't ease the discomfort in any way. Over the months I noticed my toes would point away from my knee during these bouts of boyhood trauma. I further discovered I could make the pain happen if I just pointed my toes in a certain way. (This is actually a stupid thing to do!) I now liken this to men who crush beer cans on their foreheads. "Hey look everyone, I can cause myself pain, but I am man enough to handle this pain." Some time later, in a flash of logic, I found that during such a cramp, if I manually pulled my toes toward my knee the pain would instantaneously vanish. If only I had thought of that at a much younger age!

One decade hence I was an upperclassman at Cal Poly Pomona, taking a couple of classes with a fellow student named Chi Chang Reel. She held seven world records in track and field and hailed from the Island of Taiwan.

In 1981, a dozen more years had passed. Approximately sixty of my Track and Field athletes were warming down by jogging a few laps. Suddenly I heard a loud shout. Greg Thomas, the California Interscholastic Federation champion sprinter, had fallen to the ground in obvious pain. I knew exactly what to do. I pushed his toes toward his knee and told him to get extra potassium into his body, possibly by eating more bananas. Literally seconds later, on the opposite side of the track, the scenario played itself out again, this time to Chris Crisman, an excellent hurdler.

Things went well that year and I was asked to coach an American all-star west coast track team in, of all places, Taiwan. A great deal of media converged when we landed, but most or all of them were looking to get pictures of the senator slated to greet us, the beautiful Chi Chang Reel. There we were, exiting the plane thousands of miles from home, and the absolute center of attention, the Taiwanese senator greeting us, was my college friend Chi!

Several days later at their National Invitational Track Meet, I met many people, including Ducky Drake, the only trainer in the world whose name I actually knew. UCLA's Drake Stadium was named after him.

Chris, who had just graduated from Poly High School, had run the high hurdles, but they were the High School High Hurdles (36 inches). Here he had to run the College Highs (same as Olympic, 39 inches). He was ahead, but fell over the sixth hurdle. He got up and finished. When I saw him after Ducky and his team fixed him up, he looked like a bloody mess, but only because the trainers had painted a huge amount of Mercurochrome on each and every scrape. If he spun around, he would look like a barber's pole. I had not seen that crimson medicine used in over twenty years.

The weather turned warm and humid, but with all the distractions in the large stadium, I wasn't thinking about our team's potassium levels. I was sitting up in the announcer's booth with Chi (she had asked me to help with name pronunciation) when we heard Chris call me urgently, "Coach, Coach, Coach, you gotta come with me!" He led me through some catacombs below the stadium. I could hear the bellowing cries of our number one sprinter (a young man from San Jose) echoing through the underground labyrinth. When I finally arrived in the brightly lit room Ducky said, "No rubbing, no ice.

After a few minutes it will just go away" He was right; After several seconds or minutes of hollering and screaming, the pain would indeed subside. I looked at the young athlete writhing on the gurney with his toes pointing away and parallel to his shins. He was in complete agony. I walked over and firmly pushed the toes of each foot toward his knees. Immediately the echo chamber became silent. Wow, that little piece of knowledge has certainly taken me a long way! (Maybe someday I'll tell my grandkids how I showed Ducky Drake a thing or two.)

The next day, the last before our return home, we rented a bus and went to the beach. After lunch some of us started bumping a volleyball. A few locals joined and we began counting the bumps until the ball hit something other than air or a portion of a human. We counted in English, and then we counted in Chinese. One time I dove into a few feet of water to bump the ball back into play to keep the count alive. Our new friends were amazed; I guessed they thought that was something special. Soon it was time to go and as we walked back to our area one of our team members called out, "Coach," and threw me a Frisbee. When I caught it we heard a collective gasp. It seemed they had not seen flying discs before. They shouted something to their friends up the beach as I tossed it back. The young man caught it expertly and spun it on a few fingers.

Now about a dozen people looked on, lined up and watched closely. I must point out that there are not too many Frisbee tricks I know, but I made up one of them as an eighth grader. If a Frisbee happens to be headed straight for my head, I stand at attention with my hands at my side. When it is several yards away I put my chin to my chest as if I were going to let it sail past, then at the last possible instant I blindly whip my hand over my head, hopefully slightly faster than the speed of the disc, and catch the back end. The loud cheering brought more onlookers. The clapping started when my return toss came from behind my back. I am not certain, but I think they might have been just as fascinated if we had simply played regular catch with this sailing toy. My partner "caught" it by letting it spin on one finger and passed it to himself under one leg. Some of the thirty to forty onlookers took pictures of this impromptu show. I did not know how this would end, but everyone was having a good time. I took notice that the wind was coming in off the ocean and once I had the saucer (do you remember that the first ones were called Pluto Platters?) I turned away from everyone and threw it as hard as I could out over the ocean (at an elevation of around thirty-five degrees with the plane of the disc parallel to the horizon.) One of the boys who had joined us in volleyball actually ran into the water to go get it. I stood my ground knowing it would automatically return. When it finally did I caught it behind my back. They did not know that catching behind my back did not always work quite that well for me. They did not know I was just about out of tricks. They did not know we were just a couple of guys playing Frisbee catch. They thought they were part of a crowd watching an exhibition by two members of the American National Disc Throwing Championship Team who were probably taking a short break at the beach while on a world tour.

You may remember I had just thrown it to myself, which meant everyone was waiting to see what wonder I would perform next. I pulled my last trick out of the bag. I threw it with great force, and with as much spin as I could muster, at the sand about twenty yards in front of me, but with the leading edge tilted way up. It went down as thrown, but then, before it touched any sand, rose up to the waiting fingers of my partner. While he fanned it in preparation to do more tricks, someone called from our camp letting us know we really had to go. "Okay, that's how it will end," I thought.

I announced that we had to leave and one of the young men who had bumped the ball with us translated for those who did not speak English. The jumping crowd gathered in as we tried to make our way to the bus. From different directions we were offered small tablets and pens with the one word request, "Autograph?" I tried to tell them we were just playing, but they would have nothing to do with that. They had seen our magic and saw it as only a foretaste of what we could really do. I am certain that somewhere in Taiwan there are several little books with my autograph in them followed in Chinese with the date, the location and the probable explanation: American National Disc Throwing Champion!

****

I like mathematical debates. Such discussions usually end with one side changing over completely because the point has been proven. Non-mathematical discussions, however, usually end with neither side budging from their stance. Imagine having a debate on, say, abortion, and after a few minutes the other party says, "Wow, you are right and I was wrong! I now agree with you 100%." And they mean it! Wouldn't that be nice?

"Hey, I'm okay, but I'm in the middle of a multi-car accident and will be here for hours. I need a big favor. Can you pick up my uncle at the airport?"

"I guess so, but I don't know what he looks like."

"That's okay, neither do I, but he will be wearing a yellow shirt and green pants."

"That's good, but there could be more than one person wearing a yellow shirt and green pants."

"He will have on red sandals."

"Is there anything else?"

"That'll be enough."

I don't want to miss him or anything. What if I go to the wrong guy?

"Well, he will be listening to music. The wire to one earphone will be orange and the other teal."

"What does he look like?"

"He will be riding a purple razor scooter with red wheels that flash when they spin."

"How will I know it is really him?"

"In one hand he will be carrying a picture of a black swan and in the other some petrified wood. His flight, 755, coincidently lands in fifty-five minutes. Now trust me."

In the baggage claim area you notice a man with a yellow shirt, green pants, and red sandals. But you think it might not be the right guy as he is taller than you imagined. You look around some more just in case. When you glance back you see he is riding a purple razor with flashing red wheels. The wires to his earphones are orange to the left ear and teal to the right. But then you feel the one to the right is a little more blue than teal. Yes, yes, it is quite blue in the airport light and you feel it just can't be the right guy. He has a picture in one hand, but you had envisioned it would be larger and framed. It is a smallish picture of a black swan. In the hand guiding the razor you notice it also contains a rather old looking piece of wood. You then think, "What if this isn't even the right airport? What if there is another flight 755?"

Three thousand years ago anyone could claim to be a prophet. Since prophets of God would have an accuracy rating of precisely one hundred percent, one could easily discern between them and the fakes. Sometimes false prophets were executed, but sometimes kings supported them, largely because those kings liked what they heard prophesied. Sometimes prophets of God were killed for stating unpopular prophecies. Not much of what the false prophets said has survived the centuries, but numerous prophecies by those who never failed have been faithfully recorded and passed down through the years.

Although detractors over the centuries have admitted that Jesus fulfilled the Old Testament prophecies about the Messiah, they have also asserted that these prophecies were actually written centuries after Christ's death and resurrection. They pointed out, correctly, that the earliest known existing copy of Isaiah was from circa 1000 AD.

On the coast of the Black Sea in 1947, a boy looking for a lost goat hurled a rock into a cave. Instead of hearing the echoes of a ricocheting stone in an empty cave he heard the sound of shattering pottery. Upon investigation he discovered several large sealed pots, including the one he had probably just broken.

Inside the pots were leather manuscripts wrapped in linen. They had been placed there 68 years after the birth of Christ, but were dated as having been written approximately 125 years before his birth. Those who had placed their hope in the theory that the prophecies were written after the fact, and that Jesus was just a man, simply moved on to the next theory after the discovery.

If there were proof (in the mathematical sense) of the existence of God, every mathematician would believe He exists. If there were proof of the non-existence of God, every mathematician would believe He did not exist. Many have tried their hand at such exercises; none have succeeded.

Science is a useful tool, but when it comes to proving or disproving the existence of God, science is useless. God is beyond the bounds of science. The entire concept of science is repeatable experiments; there is no such experiment for God either way. You will just have to go search for yourself.

DISCUSSION/REFLECTION QUESTIONS

CHAPTER 27   ON TRACK TOO

0. At the beach several people wanted Jerry's autograph
    because they mistakenly thought he must be famous based
    on what they had seen with their own eyes. At the Taiwan
    airport he recognized Chi Chang because he knew her
    personally. Had the fictional story about meeting the man at
    the airport been true, would you believe the man to almost
    assuredly be the uncle? In life, are you bold enough to think
    for yourself? Are you strong enough to change your mind
    even if it is an idea or perspective your friends may think
    unpopular?

1. Do you believe that Jesus rose from the dead, is God's Son,
    and has the authority and ability to forgive your sins and give
    you eternal life? Why?

2. What carries more weight with you, those who guess at what
    must have happened or those who experienced it for
    themselves? Read Acts 2:29-32 and 3:11-15. What did the
    apostles appeal to in order to give validity to their
    statements?

3. Read Acts 1:8. What are Jesus' followers called to do? What
    had the people Jesus was talking to witnessed?

4. What have you witnessed? What experiences have you had
    with Jesus? How have you experienced the resurrection?
    Who will you share it with?

CHAPTER 28   CAT 1 (UP THE HAYSTACK)

Roelof Maurer, my father, was born in Kampen, Holland in 1902. Not my grandfather, my father. Sixteen years later he was going to college, working toward a medical position.

Back then few Americans wanted to be dairymen because of the long hours, the year-round work with no days off, and the low pay. But the word was out: America was pleading for people to come to America. Roelof Maurer decided to put his name in. One year later, two weeks before his graduation, he had to choose between the medical field in Holland and a blue-collar job in the States. He chose to become a dairyman in America.

Several decades later, he sold his half of a large dairy in Lynwood, near Hynes, now called Paramount. Our family moved to another dairy in Bloomington, California, a year later--in 1955. I was five.

One day I came home from kindergarten and, after checking in with my mom, I ran out the front door and stepped into the old red barn about forty yards from the house. Inside I saw it: our new, two-story haystack, built with several tons of bailed hay.

When taking bales from such a stack, you don't take away the top layer and then the next layer of bales. Instead you work away at one corner so that you eventually form steps. My father must have already taken some hay from this stack. The first step was a two-baler (about four feet up). I climbed right to the top of the stack, which was about six inches below the bottom of the joists. I finally became bored playing up there, so I went to the milk house, and without even asking, took what I thought was some thin rope. (It was twine commonly used to wrap newspapers.) I cut off what I thought was a long piece. I went back up to the top of the haystack and, not being a boy scout, I tied a big loop around a rafter brace using a knot one might use when tying one's shoe. The loop only hung down about four feet. I put my right foot in and, with both hands, gripped the two sides of the little string. I was swinging above the joists over the haystack on the backswing and then over a two-story drop to the cement below.

My father came in a few minutes later and told me to stop. He said the string (which I knew was really a rope) might break. I could fall and possibly get hurt. Now I had seen such things on television. I knew it would actually take a long time to wear through a rope, but because TV shows only lasted half an hour, they had to show the rope fraying on the edge of a rock and then breaking in 30 minutes or less. But my dad said that I had to stop, so I had to stop. I knew he had to work every day, all day, and that he never got a day off, ever. I actually thought he was being mean to me solely because I still got to have fun and he couldn't because he had to work all of the time.

The next day I went back up, against my father's wishes. You will never guess what happened as I was swinging. Just as my father predicted, the little string broke. (Don't worry, I lived.) Fortunately, I didn't fall down the two-story drop to cement below. I fell onto the steps of hay bales. Out of control, I curled into a ball and continued in a general downward direction. Although more hay had been used, the last step was still a two-baler. I was about to fall backward and hit my head on the cement flooring, but I hit something else instead. A box that held hay hooks was perfectly situated. My father had cautioned his sons, "Always set the hooks in this box with the pointed side down. Then if someone's boots slip on the cement no one will get hurt from the sharp points."

The box was an empty milk crate. (Milk used to come in containers called bottles, made of glass. I'm not kidding--it's true.) A wooden case would either contain twelve one-quart bottles or six half-gallon bottles. In either case, the crate held three gallons of milk. Inside were double rows of heavy-duty wire so that the bottles would not rattle against one another. At the top corners of all the cases were metal posts about the size of a one-inch high stack of quarters that rose vertically so the crates could interlock. This particular case had wires that were useless, so we used the crate to store hay hooks. Whoever had used the hay hooks last had placed them pointed side down, just as my father had instructed.

Falling through the air, (come to think of it, personally, I have always fallen through air). ...Falling, I thought I was going to hit the back of my head on cement. Instead, one of the corner posts punctured the area between the top of my vertebrae and the base of my skull. Makes me wonder how different life might have been if I had made contact one inch higher or one inch lower.

I don't think I blacked out. I got up. My head hurt, but not enough to cry...yet. I was glad I didn't seem to have any broken bones. Then I placed my left hand on the back of my neck. Blood! From my head! (Operative word "my.") Not good! Now I cried as I ran to the house. With that much blood, you've got to cry.

Once inside, I was quickly escorted into the bathroom to wash the wound, and, now that I think about it, to keep blood out of the carpeted rooms. My mother stuck my head into the little sink. Someone turned on the water; it went into the wound, came out and ran down both sides of my face. I watched the large amount of pink fluid go down the drain. There wasn't much else to look at from that particular position. My life flashed before my eyes, and when you are only five, it doesn't take long.

I suppose the extent of my injury became clear when someone said, "Better get Dad." *This*, I thought, *could not be a good sign.* But my dad did know all about 1919 Dutch medicine. In fact, he was a wizard at 1919 Dutch medicine.

They turned the water off and patted the back of my neck with a towel. Then my father came in to the small bathroom. He examined the tissue in question and announced, "Get the Balm of Peru." I was just five, but had heard and understood the expression "They shoot horses, don't they?" I had just heard my father say, "Get the bomb of Peru." I thought, *a horse breaks its leg, they kill it. A little boy breaks his head, they kill him.*

Probably some rule I had not learned yet. After all, I was only five. I wish I had calmly spoken, "No, I'll be all right! It's only a flesh wound."

My father, however, must have known what I was thinking. He showed me the tin containing stuff that looked like tar and explained that it would help heal the wound. So he put the goop on my neck, the bleeding stopped and I eventually healed. My father could have cautioned, "Son, I told you so." And he could have given me a lecture. But he figured I had learned a lesson the hard way and words would be superfluous.

A few weeks later, I turned on our black and white TV--a twelve incher—and found something unusual playing: a movie! In the *morning*! Back then we got three channels, which did not broadcast during the late night or early morning hours. Mid-morning, they used to sign on with "Peer Gynt Number 5"; evenings, they signed off with "America The Beautiful." Sometimes we would turn it on and see a "test pattern." We would say, "Hey look, it's still comin' in." But on this Saturday morning, a movie was playing! A robot movie. The inventor could control the robot via a big black box with an antenna. He would tell it to get the glass of water, and it would. But toward the movie's end, something went wrong and the robot developed a mind of its own. When the exceedingly slow-moving robot started to come after its creator, the human shot at the automaton. The bullets simply bounced off its metal covering. When he ran out of ammunition, he threw the weapon at his own project. (As if a thrown gun will disable something that deflects bullets.)

The man shouted for the robot to stop, but of course it continued. I don't know why the man didn't simply walk away from the torturously slow robot. But he didn't, and I then watched in horror while the robot squeezed him to death. I thought myself supremely courageous to continue watching as blood came out of his mouth.

When the movie ended, I went outside and began to play robot, but was not having much fun. Then I found a broomstick.

Eventually I developed a game on our gravel driveway. The game consisted of placing one end of the broomstick on the driveway and the other on my stomach. As I walked forward, the gravel divided, leaving a narrow trail marking where I had been. I made a figure eight, and then more involved designs. One of these machinations led me right past my father who was speaking with some businessmen over on the side lawn. I don't know what they were talking about, but when I walked by, my father grabbed me by the arm and said, "Son, you've got to stop because you might hurt yourself." Immediately I thought, 'Dad, I'm stronger than a pebble." But I stopped.

Now our dairy, the Elm Grove Dairy, sat on the NE corner of Cactus and Slover. A little less than half a mile north were the train tracks with only our dairy and several large orange groves on this portion of Cactus Avenue. This paved street gave us a fun, safe place to play. Oh, a few potholes pocked the surface, but few people drove here, so no one bothered to repair it.

I ventured over to the road and made a new game. With one end of the stick on the asphalt of Cactus Avenue and the other on my stomach, I would run back and forth (actually forth and back) swishing the far end, seeing how close I could come to potholes without actually touching one. I could run pretty fast and come pretty darn close, I might add.

I am not exactly certain what happened next, but while I was running south with the broomstick against my stomach, the opposite end must have just caught the lip of a pothole. The broomstick came to a sudden and immediate stop. I, on the other hand, kept right on running. The small blunt end did not break the skin but did go deep into my little five-year-old body. The shock of being hit with such force and in such a concentrated area (probably my stunned diaphragm) not only caused sudden and immediate pain to my lower torso but it also expelled a massive portion of the air from my tiny little lungs.

Did you know that without air you can't cry? So I ran to my father and said...well, did you know that without air you can't talk either? But my father, knowing just about all one could know about 1919 Dutch medicine, and knowing his youngest son, and knowing what that number four son had been doing just minutes before, struck a solid blow to the area between my shoulder blades. Although it did not lessen the pain in my stomach, it (gratefully) caused my lungs to re-inflate.

He wordlessly forgave me. He did this many times in his life. I wish I could say I remember them all. Thanks Dad.

DISCUSSION/REFLECTION QUESTIONS

CHAPTER 28   CAT 1 (UP THE HAYSTACK)

0. Can you recall a time you purposefully disobeyed a parent and later wished you had not? Do you think your parents set rules for you out of love or out of stubbornness, as Jerry thought?

1. In what ways is this story a parable of your own relationship with God? What lessons can you take away from it?

2. Have you ever experienced forgiveness the way Jerry experienced it? Do you feel forgiven today? Read Psalm 103. How is God described? What is promised? Is anything required?

3. How do we respond to God's forgiveness? Does His forgiveness give us permission to continue disobeying? Explain. What can we do to show our appreciation for and understanding of God's forgiveness? Read Luke 7:36-50 and then Ephesians 4:32 and John 14:23-24.

4. Read John 1:9-13. Just as Jerry's dad offered forgiveness and healing, God the Father offers the same to His children. Are you one of His children? If you would like to become one of God's children, go to the prayer for salvation at the end of this book.

CHAPTER 29   CAT 2 (DOWN TO THE WIRE)

(RE: c1956)

The school bus stopped at the corner of Cactus and Slover, right at our dairy. While waiting for it to arrive, I would throw rocks at a telephone pole across the street about thirty yards away. If I missed, the rock would go harmlessly into an orange grove. If I hit it, I would then throw at the next pole down toward the east. When I made contact there, I would aim for a third pole much farther away. Several hours each month (times a good chunk of my growing up years) made me one pretty good rock thrower. After years of practice, I would go for the cycle with only three rocks thrown in rapid succession. Hit the close one, then the mid-range pole, then the long shot. Somewhere along the line I thought about how much fun it might be to throw at a moving car, but since I knew I'd get into big trouble, I stuck to my stationary objects.

Life on the dairy came with much work, but also plenty of memories. One memory was of the rather large number of people who would dump their unwanted cats and kittens off out front in the ivy. The dolts would then speed off. I imagine they thought they were doing us a favor, thinking, "Surely they must need more cats to catch mice in the barn and lick up spilled milk." Well, why didn't they just pull into our driveway and ask? The truth was, we already had enough cats and we did not spill milk very often. And we could not have animals running around the milk house and expect to keep our license. Once cats were dumped, someone else's problem suddenly became my father's problem. It was completely and utterly unwarranted, and happened with a sickening frequency. The dumpers were too cheap to have their pets spayed or neutered, too irresponsible and lazy to try to find homes for them, and too cowardly to take them to the pound. I considered these evil strangers as useless to society as a dead spider is to a homesick Eskimo.

This is why I started the habit of throwing rocks on selected Saturday mornings. Since Slover Avenue only saw a handful of cars an hour. I would hide a few rocks by "the umbrella tree."

(We did not know what kind of tree it was, but you can guess its shape.) Then when I saw a car coming from the east, I would hide behind that tree. In most cases the vehicle would drive right on by, but every now and then on a Saturday morning in Bloomington, California, the car would stop right in front of our Elm Grove Dairy sign by the ivy. The passenger door would open, someone would dump some kittens, the door would shut, and the car would drive off. Whereupon I would leap from behind the tree with a rock in either hand. I would try to hit the car twice, once with a line drive, easy, and again with a long parabolic trajectory, not as easy. It doesn't get any better than that.

I had it all planned. Should the weaklings summon enough courage to foolishly return in a slimy attempt to inform my father that I had hit their stupid car with rocks, I would reply, "Well, yes Dad, but they dropped off those cats." And they would be in trouble, not me. Yes, I had it all planned. No one ever returned.

My mother's brother-in-law, my Uncle Jim, knew about the continual cat problem and that my father was forced to take care of something that resulted directly from another's carelessness and subsequent cowardliness. He knew that at the pound, now called "the Humane Society," animals were kept for a while and then placed in a large metal drum for extermination. Well, imitating this system, my Uncle Jim fashioned a large, rectangular wooden box, which could be hooked up to a car's exhaust.

One sunny and cool morning he brought the box to our dairy, connected it to the tail-pipe of his car, and turned on the engine. I remember that despite the chill outside, I only wore a t-shirt, (t-shirts were always simply white back then.) Gathered around the new box were my father, my Uncle Jim, my sixteen-year-old brother Ralph, my fifteen-year-old brother Jim, a friend of my brothers, and me, age six. I thought my father would say I was too young and would have to go into the house with my mother, but he didn't. I couldn't believe it! I thought, *Here I am! I get to stay and see. This is going to be great. I don't have to go into the house like a little boy. I get to be out here. I'm a...MAN now!*

Inside the box crouched a tabby that someone had just dropped off; it seemed to be four or five months old. We stood in a semi-circle, each facing the box on the dirt just west of the milk house, as we listened to the hum of my uncle's car. I was still concentrating on containing myself at being here with all the tall men; I didn't want to blow it. Eventually my father asked, "You think it is about time?" My uncle looked at his watch and declared, "Nope, let's give it a bit longer." (As if he knew the timetable for a homemade kitty gas chamber.) Finally my uncle suggested (but with authority), "Let's turn it off and give a listen." Silence. They decided we should wait a few more minutes, a hard task for someone who was still short of seven.

I don't remember who lifted the lid. I do know it wasn't me; I didn't want to touch it. All was quiet. Stone quiet. Until a screech reverberated from within the box, followed by an escaping flash--which darted away blindly and, like a run-away radio-controlled car, smacked headlong into a tall pole. Without so much as a stunned pause, it backed up, turned a tad left, and raced across Cactus Avenue into the Zimmerman's orange grove.

Filled with questions, I blurted them out: "What was that? Is it okay? Why did it hit the pole? Where is it going? How will it find its way back?"

We never saw that box again. Not so for the cat. A few days later it returned with a funny look in its eyes and covered in foxtails. I carefully removed them. It must have been so glad to be home. It purred more than all our other cats combined. We never named this cat, but it became one of the six friendliest cats in the Northern Hemisphere, guaranteed. I think everyone felt sorry for it.

Many cats like to rub against your legs, as did this one. Cats must instinctively know to desist in this action once you start walking. This cat could not remember that important detail, so walkers had to watch foot placement near this feline.

Several weeks later the Comstock boys (a pair of twins from Paramount) came to visit my brothers Ralph and Jim. For fun, the foursome decided to sleep on an outdoor haystack about a hundred yards from the house.

In the morning, Ralph was first to rise and jumped the eight or so feet down to the ground. Well sir, those were his true intentions. Somewhere in mid-flight the cat decided it would run and greet my brother. The cat made good on his decision. My brother was already committed. Good news: my brother was not harmed or hurt in any way. Yes, good news for my brother, indeed.

A few days later, the cat returned. It must have been glad to be back home. I saw a small streak of dried blood leading from its mouth. Like Garfield, its eyes seemed to bulge more than normal. I am guessing my brother's landing broke one or two of the cat's ribs, since it now walked like a four-footed John Wayne. I think everyone felt sorry for it.

Sometime later, on a certain blue-sky-white-fluffy-cloud day in 1956, this almost seven-year-old found himself in the pen immediately east of the milk house, where no horses, no cows, and no bulls were allowed. The grass stood just below waist-high on a tallish, thin second-grader-to-be. I pulled up a big clump of grass. Dirt and roots were at one end and grass tips at the handy end. I had developed a game where I would whirl the clump around and around with increasing speed in a vertically oriented circle. If I let go at just the right time the all-natural dart would fly about as high as the huge eucalyptus trees at the northern end of our property. The impact with the ground and resulting dirt clod explosion was mesmerizing, especially if you were almost seven and, most assuredly, if you were the one who made it happen. After I'd hurled a myriad of flung projectiles, my father saw what I was doing. I thought for certain he was going to say, "Son, you have to stop because you could hit a helicopter" (or something). But he didn't say anything, so I continued playing. Soon, I mined a clump that exposed a piece of barbed wire about eight or ten feet long. I pulled it out of the grass and started to bring it to my father as I thought he might be able to use it.

While walking through the grass toward the milk house with the barbed wire trailing behind, I looked back and noticed a perfect, narrow crease in the tall grass, as if someone had parted it with a comb. I figured it would be fun to play with this before I handed it over to my father. I had already made a circle and then a figure eight when my father figured out what I was doing. He said I had to stop because I might cut my hand. But I knew I was stronger than a blade of grass. My father had to go back to work, so I started to run with wire in tow. Strands of grass began to build up on some of the individual barbs as they caught and broke. Then, I suspect, more than one barb must have become entangled simultaneously and the entire length came to a sudden and immediate halt. I, however, kept right on running.

Knowing that my father knew all about 1919 Dutch medicine and that he had told me not to drag the barbed wire, I ran straight to my mother. She whisked me to that infamous bathroom sink and ran water over my hand. She pushed the hanging flesh chunks back into their rightful places, patted off the water/blood mixture, and placed several Band-Aid bandages on my naughty little hand. (You can still see the scars.)

She then asked me how it happened. I looked at my hand. I looked at my mother. I stared at my hand and said, "The cat did it." My mother replied, "Oh that cat. Now you go out and play."

I couldn't believe it. I thought: *I'm off the hook. I disobeyed my father, got hurt and now I am not in trouble. This is the best. 'The cat did it.' I'm gonna lie from now on. 'The cat did it.' This is great.* " Life was good.

That night we had something for dinner that we only had a few times a year: creamed tuna on toast. We set up the toaster right in the middle of the dinning room table. As the toast popped up and I reached for it, my father asked, "What happened to your hand, Son?"

Before I could answer, my mother replied, "The cat did it."

To which my father slowly informed us, "We'll have to destroy that cat in the morning."

I knew what destroy meant. He was going to kill it. This was bad. He was going to kill the cat because of a lie. *My* lie. How could this turn into something so dark, so fast? As we were clearing the table, it got worse. He said, "Son, you'll have to help me in the morning." He had never said anything like that to me before. This was terrible. It got even worse as my options sank in. Either he, now we, would kill the cat for something it did not do. Or I would tell my father I lied, that I am a liar. What would my father do if I informed him I had lied? "You liar! What type of person lies to his own mother? You are the Maurer who lied. Get out of this house and never come back." Grim either way. (Of course I now know what I should have done. I should have run away from home. Yeah, that's what I should've done. That would have shown 'em.)

My mind was not made up as I fell asleep that night. When my father woke me in the morning, the black and foggy pre-dawn felt like an omen. I had never been up this early before. My father had never come in to my bedroom to wake me up before. I did not know what to do. I pretended to go back to sleep. But when my father returned a few minutes later, he made certain I was awake; he stood near my bed and waited for me to get dressed. When you are not yet seven, it takes a long time to tie your shoes, especially when you are simultaneously and desperately trying to solve the hardest problem you will probably ever have to solve in your whole entire life.

The yard was lit by a single yellow bulb (yellow, supposedly to keep bugs away.) My father handed me the flashlight and told me to call the cat. All of our cats slept by the water heater, where it was warm. I knelt down by the entrance to the crawl space and, with the aid of the light, saw all of them about a dozen feet away. "Here kitty, kitty, kitty." They remained by the water heater, except the condemned cat, the one that trusted me. It willingly came directly to me. Such a good cat. I stood and it began purring loudly while licking the right side of my neck with its soft sandpaper tongue.

My father instructed me to "turn on the hose." Which of course meant, "Turn on the water." Which meant he was going to drown it! Not good. My father and the nozzle stood at the far end of the long, heavy, industrial red hose, off in the darkness somewhere. I could hear the water hit the bottom of the empty metal bucket. I could hear water hitting water and then the continual pitch change. How I wished those deadbeats had not dropped off this cat. How I wished I had told my mother the truth in the first place. "Okay, turn it off." Of course I turned it the wrong way. "No, the other way." he corrected.

In the darkness I literally used the hose as a guide to find my father. We were all far away from the solitary yard light. With the cat still purring and licking my neck, I looked up at my father. I looked at the large, full bucket. I looked at the cat. I looked at my father. My father looked at me. I looked at the cat. My father looked at the cat. I look at the bucket. My father looked at the bucket. The cat looked at the bucket. The cat looked at me. I looked at the cat. We all looked at the bucket. This was bad. I did not know what to do, but I had to do something. I took the cat in two hands and with my face down, raised it toward my father. As he must have done a hundred times before, he put his hand on my head, mussed my hair, and said, "That's okay, Son. That's okay."

My father knew the truth all along. He wanted to test his son's mettle—then help him develop it. I wanted the cat to substitute for me for what I had done wrong. I didn't know that two thousand years earlier someone had already given His life for all the bad things I had done.

See epilogue Chapter 29

DEVOTION/DISCUSSION QUESTIONS

CHAPTER 29   CAT 2 (DOWN TO THE WIRE)

0.   Jerry knew he should not throw rocks at cars, but he rationalized that for *these* cars it would be okay. Was it okay? Are *you* rationalizing something wrong into something okay?

1.   Why did Jerry lie? With the cat's life on the line, why didn't Jerry "come clean" and confess?

2.   Define sin (Genesis 3 and Genesis 4:7 may help). How can sin be like the blades of grass in this story? How is Jerry's dad like our Heavenly Father? What other analogies and lessons about sin can you find in this story?

3.   In an effort to cover up his disobedience and protect himself from shame, Jerry was willing to sacrifice an innocent and beloved cat. To what lengths have you gone, or are you willing to go, to cover up your sin? Is it possible your Heavenly Father knows the truth?

4.   Read 1 Peter 2:23-25. A big difference between Jesus and the cat is that only one of them volunteered. Does that make a difference? Explain. Read Ephesians 2:1-10 and John 3:16-21. Covering up our sin will never succeed. What is the solution? What must you do to embrace this solution?

CHAPTER 30   Cat 3   (TOP OF THE TOWER)

(Re: April 15, 1995)

Can you call someone a friend whom you have heard speak for ninety minutes and talked to for less than thirty minutes on two separate occasions? One friend of mine according to that criteria, with the unlikely name of Hananiah Zoe, lived in Liberia, in a village called Sannaquellie.

He and his brother lived in this mostly Muslim country with their families. Even to speak of Christianity with a Muslim is strongly discouraged. Trying to convert a Muslim is considered treason. Sometimes Christians are killed for being Christians, while many around the world look away.

One particularly powerful militant Muslim wished the worst for all non-Muslims but had to settle for harassing, torturing, and killing Christians in his home country, Liberia. General Mohamed Fofana began launching random and infrequent rocket-propelled grenades into Hananiah's openly Christian village on April 15, 1995. Fofana had surrounded the village; he and his men dealt with villagers individually as they attempted to escape.

They launched grenades sporadically for two days. So far, the Zoe family had remained untouched. Then the militants caught Hananiah's brother and family. When his captors found that his prisoner had attempted to convert some Muslims, the general announced, "You tell your Jesus that I, General Mohamed Fofana, killed you." The slitting of his throat made no sound.

A few years later at a huge mosque in Monrovia, Liberia, an estimated crowd of over thirty thousand Muslims waited outside in the cooling air to hear the Friday evening prayers. With nearly two thousand inside the mosque, General Mohamed Fofana was stationed at the highest place, preparing to lead the crowd in prayer. This was not the first time he had done so, but it would be the last.

From the minaret he bellowed, "Allahu Akbar!" (God is [the] greatest.) The phrase was used this time as a call to prayer. When he finished shouting it to each of the four directions, the throng settled and quieted.

The expected seconds of silence before prayer stretched into minutes. Curious thoughts of listeners became whispers. No one knew what was happening, most especially General Mohamed Fofana. He had curved his hands around his lips as a small, impromptu megaphone to broadcast his prayer, but when he tried to speak, nothing came out of his mouth. Assistants ushered the general down and attempted to help him. It was an awkward scene; the man chosen to offer the Friday evening prayer could not make a sound. Thousands were waiting. Probably embarrassed, but definitely willing to try again, Fofana again raised his hand to his mouth. This time sound burst forth, and he shouted, "Jesu Allah! Jesu Allah!" Which means, "Jesus is God!" Something no Muslim believes. They believe Jesus was a prophet, but certainly not the Son of God, nor God himself. The situation had suddenly gone from awkward, to Muslim blasphemy and, therefore, treason.

An important leader in Monrovia and, by no small coincidence, the general's father, was quickly summoned. When the father heard what had happened, he declared for all within earshot, "You are no longer my son, forever! You are a traitor!" Right then and there they stripped Fofana of his uniform and most of his clothes. They took his weapons and ammunition. In less than a minute he went from a powerful general who gave orders to countless men, to a man with nothing. No father, no clothes, no weapons, no place to go. Fofana had come to the mosque prepared to lead evening prayer and had left in shame.

He wandered with no purpose, no direction. He eventually found himself at a small but well-known Christian corner. A few Christians helped him and decided to take him to their pastor: Hananiah Zoe. Neither man knew the other. Hananiah gave him a pair of his own shoes and some clothes. Hananiah ministered to this man with actions and when asked, with words. A Muslim living in a Christian's home, Fofana finally explained who he was. After a few weeks of questions, answers, and logical deduction, Hananiah figured out that his guest was the man outside Sannaquellie years earlier, the one responsible for the death of many Christians, and that he had personally killed his host's brother! Zoe was dumbfounded. At first he wanted revenge, but gradually remembered the antidote for grief to be grace. The two spoke for endless hours. Fofana explained that when he was at the top of the tower, he became mute from shock when there in front of him he saw the clear image of Jesus Christ.

After hearing Mohamed Fofana tell his personal story, many have joined him in his enthusiasm for Christ. Fofana went from taking the lives of Christians to showing people how to give their lives to Christ. I claim he is far more powerful now than he ever was.

My father continually showed me grace: the string over the haystack, the broomstick on the street, the barbed wire in the field, the disappointment he must have felt when his young son failed to own the truth on a dark, foggy morning. Mohamed Fofana received absolutely no grace from his father, but a full-blanketing forgiveness from his Father in Heaven.

See epilogue Chapter 30

DEVOTION/DISCUSSION QUESTIONS

CHAPTER 30   Cat 3   (TOP OF THE TOWER)

0. Hananiah Zoe forgave Mohamed Fofana for killing his brother. How might this story be different if he had not? How might Hananiah's life be different if he had not forgiven him?

1. What astonishes you about this story?

2. Read Luke 19:9-10. What did Jesus identify as His mission? Is it possible to accomplish this mission without forgiveness? Explain.

3. Read Matthew 6:12-15 and Matthew 18:21-35. Given what you have already learned about Jesus' mission, why is it so important to Jesus that His followers forgive others?

4. Do you agree or disagree with this statement. "The Good News of Jesus Christ is most powerful and convincing when people see and experience forgiveness." Explain the reasons for your answer. Is there someone you are struggling to forgive? Often we struggle to forgive because our focus is behind us, on the person and the harm they caused, rather than ahead of us, on Christ and what He wants to do in our lives. What can you gain from forgiving? In order to find the motivation to forgive, focus on what you will gain and not on what you will surrender.

CHAPTER 31   DIXIE

(RE: 2001)

The philosopher said, "If one holds too tightly to the past, his arms won't be free to embrace today." To which his father answered, "True, but do not let your precious memories be stolen by time."

My sister Dixie was born July 12, 1946. When she was eight and I was five, our brother Jack was set to marry Barbara Dalrymple of the Washington Dalrymples. They asked me to be the ring bearer and Dixie to pass out "The Groom's Cake." I had no inkling what either meant.

Imagine yourself five years old—and hearing that you will be (read slowly) "The Ring Bear." Feel the change in emotion when you discover that to accomplish this important task you must wear a suit and tie! Remember that you are five! Imagine the shock when you learn from your sister you will probably walk on white paper and carry a white silk pillow with a diamond ring on it. Further consider the horror when you discover the pillow will be dainty, the ring will be safety-pinned to the pillow, and the ring itself will be fake. Let the word "dainty" sink in. Now recall that the operative word from moments ago was "bear."

Our parents drove with the two of us from Southern California northward in the family's white Chrysler. There wasn't much to do on highway 99. When Dixie mentioned that hundreds of people would be watching me, I became nervous. She asked, "Can you walk and carry a pillow at the same time?" I said, "Yes, that is all I have to do; walk and carry a pillow." She was right, that was all that I had to do.

While on the seemingly much longer trip home, I asked Dixie, "Why do they call our brother 'Jack' when we are in California and 'John' when we are in Washington?" She explained as best she could, but what I really wanted to know was what they called him in Oregon.

We spoke of many things for all those hours, most of which I have forgotten, but I do remember how we wondered if it would hurt to die. I was afraid of death. If it hurt when you burned your finger, how much worse must it hurt when your whole body died? Years later, we each became enamored with what the Good News stood for, and neither of us feared death again.

The day before my first day of seventh grade, Dixie must have noticed I was apprehensive. She reasoned, "All your brothers and sisters made it just fine through Junior High, and all of your friends from sixth grade will be there, just like you. You'll do fine."

Four decades later, Dixie was diagnosed with an inoperable cancer that surrounded her internal organs. I will let excerpts from some selected emails tell this beautiful story.

(Jerry writing in June 2001)

Dixie told me she has been so blessed, and then she named the blessings, concluding with, "Mike [her husband] has made me feel (then she literally placed her hand to her heart while she searched for the truth)...cherished!" She continued, but I don't know what she said. The word "cherished" and the way she had said it, remained....I will not forget that moment of our lives.

Saying goodbye to my sister was....I have no word for it. Standing there, holding one another, crying, trembling, knowing we probably would not see one another on earth again. Little kids on a dairy, in school, growing up, dating, getting married, having children, praying together....

(Dixie writing)

Thank you, Dear Ones, for your prayers and encouragement. I truly am resting on the work of your prayers. I feel armed and ready to face the enemy!

(Later she wrote this)

The first one [chemotherapy] went well--only 10 minutes, no problems. The second one "Etoposide" began, but almost immediately I suffered a severe reaction. The nurse called for the doctor, Mike told me to breathe and Julie [their daughter] reminded me to pray. As soon as I called the name of Jesus out loud, my nurse began praying out loud, called a second nurse and said, "We have family praying here." And she began praying also. God truly provided "angels" all around! I only learned later that both Mike and Julie thought I was dying and that they were saying good-bye to me. It was an intense 5 minutes! And every one in the oncology unit came to see the one who suffered the "Etoposide reaction."

Dear Ones, (Dixie writing on Saturday, 7/14/01)

And Disneyland is still in the works! Another friend, knowing I needed some extra padding for the wheelchair, covered a chair pad in Disney characters! [Disneyland was arguably one of Mike and Dixie's favorite places.]

Dear Ones, (Dixie writing on Monday, 7/16/01)

My oncologist called and told me my blood count is way down and I shouldn't risk crowds. I'm all packed for Disneyland and this is a huge blow. We finally allowed ourselves the joy of this trip and now it is a big risk factor.

Dear Ones, (Dixie writing on Friday, 7/20/01)

Mickey and Minnie are well and send their greetings.

Thanks to your prayers and God's grace, we enjoyed a wonderful visit to Disneyland. I was quite comfy on the drive there (8 hours) and back. Our hotel room was directly across from the Magic kingdom so the twins rode on my lap on the wheelchair until we rented their strollers. It was quite a sight—me, with my wide brim safari hat I had purchased last year for my trip to the Holy Land, holding a pink umbrella and the twins.

We loved all the rides and only had one really scary one. On Wed. night, while in line to see Winnie the Pooh and Tigger, we lost Abby. It was dark, we were worried and the boys were crying. So while Scott, Julie and Mike searched for Abby, the boys and I prayed. Forty-five minutes later at the lost children's office, we were reunited with our granddaughter. The best part of the story, other than finding her safe, was who found her. A woman who was there with her children and mother found Abby. When they notified security, the officer insisted on taking Abby. But that lovely woman followed him all the way back to Main Street and then waited until we arrived to see that Abby was safe. When she heard that the boys and I had been praying, she told us she also was a Christian. God protects and provides!

My favorite memory of this vacation, and there are too many to list, happened on the second morning. My high school sweetheart and husband of almost 38 years stopped pushing my wheelchair and asked me to dance--right there on Main Street. Through tears of sadness at not being able to grow old with him and tears of joy at the life we've shared, together we danced. It will be my favorite dance for all time.

I thank God for the energy and protection He gave me. I ate dinner with the family and we stayed at Disneyland until after 10 PM, with only one trip to the hotel room for lunch and nap about noon. The fireworks in the evening were spectacular and I think they may be a pale glimpse of what Heaven will be like.

After thanking God, I thank each of you who prayed us through this week. We could not have done it without you! I enjoyed this trip against my doctor's advice, ate regular food, went on most of my favorite rides (Small World, Jungle Boat), saw the joy and wonder of this special place in the faces of five of my grandchildren and returned safely. WOW!

And now it's over and I am still learning to live with cancer. My hair is falling out. I didn't think it would bother me, but it does. And it's such a nuisance! Have you ever put on lotion or Chap Stick and then have your hair fall out and stick to you? I'll have to learn in a hurry how to do those turbans and wigs. Hope I don't scare anyone.

Dear Ones, (Dixie writing on Saturday, 7/28/01)

Last night I gave Mike his bi-monthly hair cut. His usual--a buzz cut all over. When we were finished, it was his turn. He gave me the same haircut. Friends said I look like a "Chia Pet Grammy."

It's only hair, but somehow it's really important when it's MY hair. I've given my hair to the Lord, but I did cry the night before while making the decision. Sometime next week my friend will shave my head completely. This gives me (and my family) a little time to adjust. I just don't want to scare anyone. I still get startled when I look in the mirror without thinking.

(Jerry writing on 8/1/1)

She said sometimes when she was at the bottom, and her prayer time was stalling, she needed to see the face of God to continue praying. Where could she go for that? Dixie said she went to the mirror to look into her own eyes, because she knew He was in there! And then she could pray again. Someday, you'll have to meet my sister Dixie.

(Jerry writing)

Just spoke with Dixie via phone again, as I am preparing to leave on a mission trip to South Africa tomorrow. It was her third day in a row of chemo--her second series. Our older sister, Marilyn, is there. Dixie is not experiencing nausea and said it is so great to have Marilyn there to help stay positive. She told me that every time she listens to "the" song, (Ron Perry's remake of "Lion Sleep Tonight" with Christian lyrics, A+) she pictures me mouthing the words as I had done the first time I played it for her. (I guess it was good she couldn't see me crying on the other end of the phone.) Since she needs exercise, my two sisters have started the habit of dancing to the song twice each morning. Dixie said, "The next time I have chemo, Marilyn won't be here to help me."

Marilyn responded, "Don't start getting negative." Dixie laughed. Then Dixie prayed, as Marilyn held on.......for........me! (I guess it was good they couldn't see me crying on the other end of the phone.)

(Dixie writing)

Even in the midst of all the tears and sadness, I never feel alone. That is one of God's gifts to me. He is an Awesome God and He knows my name and holds me in the palm of His hands. I can

TRUST HIM completely! How could I ever feel alone? I experience daily His love for me in the visits, cards, calls, hugs, e-mails each of you offer me. Thank you for bringing me so much love and encouragement!

"Because YOUR love is better than life, O LORD, my lips will glorify YOU. I will praise YOU as long as I live, and in YOUR name I will lift up my hands." Psalm 63:3-4

With thanks and love beyond words, from one of His children,

Dixie :)

(Jerry writing on 8/30/1)

Yesterday, Adele was on the way from the Sacramento Airport to a horse show in Grass Valley, when she stopped to visit Dixie.

Dixie said, "If you'd have been here an hour earlier, you'd have seen me throwing up." When Adele asked how she was doing now, and Dixie said, "Well let's see. My cup containing my extra-strong painkillers is empty. My cup containing my anti-depressant pills is empty, so I must be pretty good."

They had a great visit. Adele said Dixie's hair and eyebrows are starting to come in, and they are white. She said Dixie's face was gaunt and that my sister was not quite strong enough to open a bottle of Seven Up.

(Dixie writing on 9/2/1)

Enough dreary news. How's this for tender? Three year-old Anna was instructed not to hug or come near Grammy because she, Anna, had a cold. At her pouting countenance, her mother suggested that she COULD touch my feet. When we walked up to their front door, she was the first to greet me. She ran up full speed, spread her arms for a full hug but at the last minute remembered her instructions. She instantly bent down and touched my toes. Too precious.

(Jerry writing on 9/3/1)

My sister, Marilyn, has pictures of Dixie taken at the church. The praise band is practicing and no one else is there. So Dixie can be. Dixie's hat and head are tilted just right listening to her daughter, Julie, practice with the rest of the band. There are also pictures of Dixie from her pew, eyes closed, palms up, endearing smile, singing her heart out along with the band. Marilyn says Dixie still has a beautiful voice.

Jerry

(Jerry writing on 9/13/1)

I just got off the phone with Mike. The hospital bed came and it is in the living room. Mike is still working. A different person from church spends the day with her until Mike returns. The Hospice social worker stops by for a short visit twice a week. For the past two weeks Dixie has been eating tiny watermelon slices and also milk with shaved ice. Dixie is exceedingly weak. It takes most of her energy to get up to go throw up. (To throw up takes many minutes, up to twenty.) Mike said she is so weak she does not talk in full sentences when phrases will do. Instead of, "Mike, when you can find the time, could you please make a glass of shaved ice and milk?" it's, "Mike...milk." Mike says he knows that is not Dixie; it is just the way it has to be. The pain medication is working, but obviously the nausea medicine is not. They are trying a different nausea medication now.

While Mike and Dixie were talking Sunday evening, Dixie said, "I'm ready to go." Mike said he told her not to hang on for us. If she was ready to go, go ahead. (The hospice nurse has since given a timeline of about four to six weeks.) Dixie is overwhelmingly tired. Mike said Dixie is losing the battle, but has already won the war. He continued, saying she has kept her faith through all of this and is such an inspiration to him. (Mike, me, and many others.) I'm not certain, but there may be no more email messages from Dixie. I know she would write if she could.

Just before I called, Dixie told Mike she had to throw up. Mike said, "Okay." After a few minutes, Dixie said, "I guess I don't have to." Mike turned on the fan as she started to lie down. When he looked back, she was asleep.

I thought Mike might be tired of talking about Dixie, explaining repeatedly to helpers, visitors, neighbors, friends, and relatives.

I tactfully changed the subject. Mike tactfully brought it back to his wife. He checked on her; she was still sleeping. We talked for quite awhile.

Jerry

Forgive me for being so melancholy. I can just hear Dixie, in an honest effort to cheer me up, earnestly ask, "Jerry, isn't God good?" Even in these unsettling days, the answer is, "Of course, Dixie."

Jerry

(Jerry writes regarding 9/19/1)

The family was around Dixie's bed at the hospital. Dixie was very weak and therefore kept her eyes closed and said little. Loved ones were conversing quietly while Dixie slept. Mike mentioned something about paying the bills, when a tiny hoarse voice came from Dixie's direction. Dixie said slowly and deliberately, "Mortgage...payment...not...automatic." At the time, no one knew these would be her last words, thinking of others and details.

Hours later, Mike was alone with Dixie, and a little after 11 pm, Mike noticed a change in her breathing pattern. Dixie's heart was working extra hard to get oxygen to her dehydrated body. Mike said, "I love you, Hon. Why don't you go home?" Two deep breaths and she was. When it came time to tell his daughter about her mother, he couldn't. On the phone, Julie figured it out. At home, Mike couldn't tell his sister-in-law, Marilyn. Mike said, "I didn't know what to do." Marilyn said, "You're supposed to hug me." Mike later told me that the end "was beautiful."

Proud to be Dixie's little brother,

Jerry

See epilogue Chapter 31

DISCUSSION/REFLECTION QUESTIONS

CHAPTER 31   DIXIE

0. Have you had an experience similar to Jerry's--when he said
    goodbye to his sister and they both knew they would
    probably never see each other on earth again? Imagine that
    same scene between two people who do not believe humans
    have souls.

1. How do you feel about death? Do you fear it? Do you avoid
    talking or even thinking about it? Do you think you are
    prepared for it? Some people are life giving even when facing
    death, while others seem to drain the life out of everyone
    around them. Which do you think you'll be? Explain.

2. What things helped Jerry's sister prepare for and face death?
    What can you do to make sure those kinds of things are
    readily available to support you?

3. Read Revelation 21:1-5 and 1 Corinthians 15:50-56. It is one
    thing to read and know about these verses, but that won't
    comfort you. You must be confident that they are absolutely
    true. What can you do now to build that confidence so that
    you'll have it whenever the time comes that you'll need it?

4. Read John 11:21-27. What reasons do we have for believing
    this to be true?

CHAPTER 32   BROTHERS

(RE: Late 1940's and Early 1970's)

Recently four brothers--Jack, postman and missionary, retired; Ralph, risk manager for the state of California, retired; Jim, Christian Minister; and I--met for a bike ride and to reminisce. I won't tell you which was the most fun.

Jack was drafted into the U.S. Army on January 18, 1953. Fortunately they discovered his musical talent, whereby he became part of the Army band at Fort Lewis in Washington State. At the time I was four-and-a-half and about to get my tonsils removed. Of course I had been promised all the Jell-O and ice cream I wanted. On the way home from the doctor's office after the surgery, I found myself standing on the front seat between my parents and facing backward. (No seatbelts back then.) To my astonishment, my brother Jack was driving his 1952 Plymouth immediately behind us. I swallowed painfully and hoarsely whispered, "Jack." My mother replied that he was off in the Army and that we wouldn't get to see him for several weeks. I waved to my brother; he waved back. I was unable to convince either parent their oldest son was only two car-lengths away.

When we pulled into the driveway, my parents were completely surprised when Jack followed moments later. The reunion was sweet for everyone except me, standing frustrated and barefoot in my jammies on the cement. I wanted to say, "Hey! What about me, your youngest son, down here? The one who just had surgery." But the excitement was contagious; Jack was home.

In 1946 (several years earlier), when our family's dairy was on Olive (now called Alondra) near Orange, in Hynes (which was combined with Clearwater to form Paramount), CA., our father asked my older brother Ralph, "How much do you love me?" This was apparently unusual for my father, but six-year-old Ralph, without hesitating, replied, "From here to the garage, and twice back and forth in an airplane!" This so impressed those listening that they wrote it down. I still remember my father speaking of this event.

I have a third older brother, Jim. In 1948 he and Ralph were
playing atop a ground-level water-filled holding tank at the dairy.
They managed to get a bit wet and decided to dry their
sweatshirts. Instead of placing them on any portion of the
hundreds of yards of fencing, they chose to put them near a flood
lamp at the top end of the milking barn and closer to the sun--in
order to dry them more quickly. (Very logical.) After Ralph laid
his sweatshirt on the peak of the metal roof, Jim went to hang his
over the conduit that extended horizontally out to the flood lamp.
Water and electricity were not the problem. The problem was
that the arm of the fixture was only conduit and was
approximately eighteen feet above the ground. Seven-year-old
Jim began to slip. Eight-year-old Ralph grabbed his ankle. The
old conduit gave way. Within moments, Jim was hanging upside
down, suspended solely by Ralph. Things just couldn't get much
worse. Then, slowly, Ralph began to slip. No problem. He still
had two or three more seconds to make a decision. Ralph
soberly apologized in advance to his dangling younger brother
saying, "Jim, I'm sorry, but I can't hold you any longer; I have to
let you go." Looking back it was the correct thing to do. The
choice was one boy falling off the roof, or two.

On the way to the cement below, Jim hit a wooden gate,
lengthwise. Ralph hollered for Jack, who happened to be
practicing his clarinet about 30 yards away on the back porch.
Jack ran outside, jumped the fence, picked up Jim, and brought
him to the house.

When the doctor arrived, one of the first things he did was ask
Jim, "What's your name?" Ralph answered, "Jimmy!" The
doctor was trying to figure out how aware Jim was so he put a
finger in front of his own lips, and pointing to our mother, asked
Jim, "Who is this?" Ralph said, "That's Mom!"

Amazingly, Jim received no broken bones or scars to show for
the ordeal. Ralph was not quite so lucky, because we have not let
him forget that he answered for Jim when the doctor clearly
wanted Jim to answer.

Jumping to October 1972. My first year of teaching included three classes of boys PE. It was football season and I found myself running quite a bit between fields correcting difficulties. I got the bright idea to make new teams and place all the troublemakers on the same team. It actually worked well. Most problems usually occurred on one field. If the "special" team fell too far behind and lost interest, I would jump in to help them out.

In one class, however, one young man made it his goal to ruin the fun for everyone. The vice principal told me that many years before, a certain teacher had disciplined him by making him stand with his arms outstretched and a book in each hand. He suggested I give that method a try.

The next day Denny purposely wrecked another play, so I instructed him to "Go stand on the sideline, put your hands out, and just wait until I tell you to put them down." I called another play. After we ran it, I looked over and saw that he had taken off his flag belt, placed the middle of it on top of his head and held an end in each hand, thus forming a relaxing "suspension bridge." I told him to put his belt on like every one else and put his hands out horizontally. I called another play, ran it, and looked over. He had taken the top end edge of each sleeve of his t-shirt and pinched it between the thumb and curled index finger of each hand. Once he stretched out his arms he did form a rather comfortable looking "T." I told him he could not use his belt, or shirt, or shoelaces (I was thinking ahead now) to support his arms. I called another play, ran it and looked over. Denny, as instructed, had formed a cross ... flat on his back. I said nothing. I thought, "This kid thinks faster than I do." I let him lie there harmlessly for the rest of the game.

A year or two later I noticed a girl named Jennie in the back of one of my Algebra classes with her head on her desk. Knowing full well that none of my lectures could possibly be boring enough to induce sleep, I asked the class to finish the last few steps of an example problem we had been working and walked back to her desk. She was not asleep but unconscious!

Thankfully she was breathing. I asked the boy whom I thought would run the fastest to step outside. I quietly informed him this was not a drill and told him to run all the way to the nurse (a couple hundred yards away), tell her this was an emergency, and bring her here immediately. I added that if the nurse was not around he should bring an administrator (at the time my room had no phone or intercom).

The students did not know something was amiss. I made up a similar problem they could work on while I kept a close eye on Jennie. I wondered if the nurse would clear the room when she arrived. When I saw the nurse approaching in a golf cart, I met her outside and told her what I knew. She came in and helped our patient into a more comfortable position, sitting on the carpet and leaning on the back wall. The nurse signaled the class with the universal signal for silence, asked the girl for her name and I answered, "Jennie." Me, I said it! (It was hard to believe, but I had just "pulled a Ralph." I did not want to believe it. Don't tell my brothers, it would be too hard to live down. Ralph was only eight when he answered for Jimmy.)

It turned out Jennie had juvenile diabetes, but suffered no ill effects from her episode in that Algebra class. (The classrooms now have phones and computers, and teachers have access to the released medical conditions of their students.)

Oh yeah, the bike ride. That was fun too.

"I sought my soul, but my soul I could not see. I sought my God, but God eluded me. I sought my brother and I found all three."
Unknown

DISCUSSION/REFLECTION QUESTIONS

CHAPTER 32   BROTHERS

0. You know what "pulling a Ralph" means in this story. To
    your friends and family what would "pulling a 'your name
    here'" mean?

1. Read 1 Thessalonians 4:9-10 and Galatians 6:9-10. What
    does it mean to you to be part of the "family of God"? Does it
    evoke positive or negative feelings? What do you think it
    would have meant to a first century Christian?

2. How do these verses say we are to treat our brothers and
    sisters? If this is true, and it is the Word of God, why are
    there so many church fights? What would our churches be
    like if we were to put our focus on practicing these verses
    instead of exercising our "rights"?

3. Would it make a difference if you viewed everyone at your
    church as a brother or sister? Explain. Would it make a
    difference to you if the people at church loved and treated
    you as a brother or sister? If so, what kind of difference?
    Would it make a difference to the world outside the church?

4. Does anything prevent you from seeing and treating others as
    brothers and sisters in the family of God? What is something
    you can do to grow in your ability to see and treat others as
    your brothers and sisters in the family of God?

CHAPTER 33   THE DEVIL YOU SAY

(RE: March 18 – 21, 2010)

We were eighty men eating homemade cookies inside the walls of a state prison near the Mexican border. I did not know who would be at my table, but I tried to meet as many as possible of the men I did not know. I spoke at length with a man who, on the outside, had been a mechanical engineer and on the inside was a lifer. Since he resembled Dobie Gillis' father, I will call him Gillis. He was well-spoken, with a large vocabulary, and easy to converse with, but admitted having nothing in life to look forward to. He openly confessed, "If Kevorkian came right now and asked for volunteers, I would raise my hand in earnest."

After members of our team each gave a thirty-second personal introduction to the rest of the room, the inmates did likewise. The first was a six-foot-four, exceedingly thin, glasses-wearing man with a cane. He looked a bit like Abraham Lincoln with a goatee instead of a beard. I will call him Abe. Within four seconds he stumbled a few short steps to the side and then stabilized himself. Stephen, the man heading up this four-day weekend, quickly supported him. Abe, who always spoke softly in a slow cadence, informed us that he was from Rubidoux, had HIV, and was a Satanist.

At our table sat Kairos brother Thomas, Fr. Eric (an Anglican priest), I, and five of an expected six inmates. As it turned out, one could not make it and the short alternate list had been exhausted. Since more than two hundred had applied, one lucky man was about to get his wish. Rounding out the Family of John were Will, reserved but willing to share; Chris, a strong Christian; Hyper, controlling his tendencies to be continually active; Gillis, and Abe. Before long we were introduced to a happy-go-lucky young man named Haps, who would complete our team of nine.

A Kairos weekend has many activities that revolve around eleven related talks given over four days by appointed volunteers. Each of us had been given excellent outlines for the speeches; those who wrote and refined those outlines deserve an A. I had been asked to give the first one, entitled "Choices." I was not prepared for the effect it would have on some of the men. In prison many choices are made for them, but the important choices are not.

As you might imagine, there are times for group discussions and individual conversations, especially after a talk. Abe told me he liked to draw, which I knew would come in handy, because we would be making a few posters on some key points. He also said he had diabetes and colon cancer. He opened up and told me he took lots of methadone for his pain. On the second morning when it came time to draw, he said he did not feel well enough to do so. About twenty minutes later, he confessed to me that he had taken his meds, plus had shot up with illegal morphine. He said he felt as if he had let the team down. I quietly asked if he took the morphine for the pain or to get high. His rambling answer was noncommittal. I asked again, but he would not give a definitive answer. When Fr. Eric heard this from Abe he told him, "Abe, you are dying here. Now is the time to choose whether you will spend eternity with Satan in Hell or with Christ in Heaven."

Hyper felt a true compassion for Abe. Hyper told us that drugs had ruined his life too. A highlight for Hyper was getting letters from his daughter. He believed his daughter had stopped writing when he started using again.

Fifteen graduates, mostly from the previous Kairos, comprised the "inside team." They willingly helped with cookies, punch, coffee, water, sorting over three thousand pieces of "Agape mail," serving, cleaning up, and whatever else needed to be done. One of them quietly let us know that Gillis was the top dog, the man who had called all the shots in a previous yard. Gillis told Fr. Eric that he was probably the worst inmate in the room and that a combination of circumstances got him here. Fr. Eric responded, "No. You chose to do certain things. Your choices got you here."

Another man from the inside team, Cameron, had recently been stabbed by his cellie (cellmate) with a shank (home-made knife).

The cellie was placed in Adseg (Administrative Segregation, deemed "the hole" in old movies). Cameron matured more in six months than most men on the outside do in six decades. Cameron wrote a letter to his former cellie completely forgiving him for what he had done. (As Fr Eric would say, "Talk about imitating Christ!") That single action accomplished many things, one of which was to stir the warden to cut the Adseg term short.

On the third day each of the six families temporarily abandoned their tables and moved chairs to form tight knee-to-knee circles. I explained that we would not go around the circle and pray, that each man could pray once, or more times (or not at all) and in any order. A few days earlier we had been strangers, and now we were a group of humble men holding hands and praying. At Kairos our sole purpose is to listen and love. That's it. We listened to their prayers.

I should not have been surprised to hear each man pray. I should not have been shocked when Hyper asked, "What is that prayer you pray when, when ... (you want to turn your life over to Jesus)?" I should not have been amazed when I heard Hyper, Will, Haps, and Abe repeat the words as Fr. Eric lead the sinner's prayer!

Later Hyper again told me that drugs had ruined his life and he really wanted to quit. He said he had tried before and knew it would be hard. Eventually he and I went outside to talk alone. He asked what he should do. I gave a little advice that seemed logical to me and then said I should find someone to help him who knew more about quitting drugs than I did. He insisted that I tell him what to do. He said the temptation would be strong and knew he would struggle with it. The advice poured out of me, one thing after another that he could do. Hyper's eagerness and encouragement had made my confidence soar. He said he really wanted to make it this time and I said I wanted to hear a good report next Saturday. His face sported an instant smile and his eyes grew wide. He swung his right hand out and then vigorously back to shake mine. "You're gonna be here next Saturday? That's what I needed to hear!"

Back inside, Abe asked for my advice on quitting drugs, as he did not want to talk to a member of the clergy. I only had time to give him the short version. At the end of the day, I advised first Hyper and then Abe that their job was to "just make it until tomorrow morning--tomorrow morning."

Sunday morning came with good news from Abe and Hyper. Gillis, however, told the table he wished he could ditch drugs, but that he could not bring himself to toss his outfit (equipment needed to take drugs). He knew he was in charge and could make a commitment to quit if he chose.

Soon the conversation turned to the Agape letters they had received the day before. The men wanted to tell which letter had meant the most. For Will it was the one from "a new mother with a tiny baby's footprint in ink." For Hyper it was the letter from an eleven- year-old who told him he could change if he wanted to. Gillis said he hadn't cried in thirty years, but did so reading these letters. I believe they all cried while reading their mail. They took each message as a sign that someone actually cared about a forgotten man.

When the topic changed and we were laughing again, Gillis placed his thumb and index finger at the corners of his mouth and said, "I've smiled so much in the past few days these muscles actually ache." A little later he said he now had something to look forward to. That's a long way from hoping for a visit from Kevorkian!

More than one man said he had "never felt love like this" and that they could tell it was real. Slowly Abe revealed "Every priest I had spoken with wanted nothing to do with me once I informed him I was a Satanist. And now (pointing to Fr. Eric) this man is like my best friend." A lot can change in four days.

Approximately thirty visitors joined us for our closing ceremony. Speakers made some great points, but when slow-walking, slow-talking Abe went to the open mike, his short, matter-of-fact statement caused a standing ovation. He said, "Satan can go to hell."

The names were changed, but not to protect the innocent. None of us were.

DISCUSSION/REFLECTION QUESTIONS

CHAPTER 33   THE DEVIL YOU SAY

0. Being a Christian gets you no points outside and especially
    inside prison. Being a Christian, or a Muslim, or an atheist
    (etc.) in prison gets you no points with the parole board.
    Besides the cookies, why do you think so many inmates want
    to get into the Kairos program?

1. Are you the type of person who is quick to listen *or* quick to
    give advice? Would your friends agree? Which type of
    person would you prefer to open up to?

2. Read 1 Corinthians 13. Paul distills the essentials of life down
    to three things: faith, hope and love. Do you agree? Would
    you change the list? Could you survive if you had faith in
    nothing? How about if you had no hope or love?

3. Why do you think love is considered the greatest of the three?
    Jerry said that his job was simply to listen and to love. It
    obviously had an impact, but that was in a prison. Could just
    listening and loving (and only offering advice when asked)
    have as powerful an impact in the outside world? Explain.

4. Which is harder for you to do: to listen without quickly
    jumping in with comments and advice, or to love without
    judging someone who is not loveable? Try an experiment.
    See if you can have greater influence on someone's life by
    listening more, speaking less, and showing more compassion
    and love. What is something you can do to remind yourself
    to hold your tongue and listen next time you're having a
    conversation? What is something you could do to remind
    yourself to find some way of showing love to that person
    (possibly even tangible)?

CHAPTER 34   KAIROS 84

October 25, 2010

Kairos 84 ended yesterday afternoon and now I sit in the jury waiting room in Vista hoping they don't want me. Imagine, hoping not to be wanted.

Five of us on the Kairos outside team, who drive a little farther than most of the others, sleep in a sixth grade classroom in the elementary school at the St. John Episcopal Church in Chula Vista, not too far from R. J. Donovan California State Correctional Institute. We bring our own sleeping gear. One uses a cot, one uses a Futon, and the rest of us use air mattresses. I use a large one and an old black and white tuxedo-clad penguin comforter. I wish I could say I slept like a log, but each of the four days saw me a little more tired than the previous. We could afford hotel rooms, but then we would miss the nightly recaps and camaraderie.

On the previous Saturday we had passed out invitations to some of those who had applied. I was randomly paired with Rev. Edward, a former inmate of this very prison yard and graduate of Kairos many years earlier. Few can match the effect of his testimony on those imprisoned here. We were assigned to deliver the good news to the gym, a makeshift "cellblock" with inmates given bunks in stacks of two or three. As soon as we entered the noisy room, an occupant eager to help met us with a smile (he knew we were passing out invitations to Kairos). When I got to the last envelope I asked if he knew Cleat Stout. His answer was a gigantic smile. *He* was Cleat Stout. He told us he was getting out in a month and a half and he had prayed hard that he would be invited.

Thursday was the first day, when we finally got to meet the candidates we each were sponsoring. Crew told me that he had received the letter I had sent him earlier. I soon learned that

Crew had left Christianity years earlier, and turned to Islam. A "180."

At each of the six tables sat three men from the outside and six from the inside. At my table the other two outside men were Rev. Edward and a young man named Michael, who, with the help of God, had turned his life completely around.

Many of the inmates take some form of medication. Three of the thirty-six men, who were chosen from a large pool of applicants, were so heavily medicated (either legally, illegally, or a combination thereof) that their faculties were greatly dulled. I'm guessing it was no coincidence that two of these men were at our table. At first I thought other applicants who were not so dependent should use these spots, but my attitude slowly and reluctantly changed. My friend Anthony summarized this concept in one short sentence: "You don't bring sand to the beach!"

We shared, discussed, listened, laughed, and prayed together for four days. Ty, solid and six-foot-three, also sat at our table. He shared with me how good it felt to call his wife and tell her what he had learned. She has been in "Kairos Outside" for eight years and has been praying for him all that time. When he told her some of the things he had experienced in these last few days, she could only cry. When it hit him how much she loved him and how much he had missed by not opening up, Ty cried too.

Also at our table was Cleat, the man who helped Rev. Edward and me get the invitations delivered in the gym. He told how he had been dragged to church as a kid, but rejected everything about it by age thirteen. He volunteered that his grandmother, whom he obviously loved, said if he kept going down the path he had chosen, he would go to prison and she would die while he was locked up. He assured her that wouldn't happen. He freely recounted some of his crimes, but also told how he had risen to a position of responsibility while incarcerated. Then he explained that while still a prisoner, he had been entrusted with driving a state vehicle outside the yard, and that when he learned that his grandmother had died, he went to see her without permission (also know as escaping from prison). When caught, he was put in "the hole." On May 7, 2006, while in that cell, he turned his life over to Christ! The guards thought he was alone. He wasn't.

Shorty on the other hand, was even more stubborn. For the Kairos in a row, I gave the first talk, entitled "Choices." During that talk I mentioned that I taught at a high school in Riverside. Immediately afterward, Shorty, who sat next to me at our table, could hardly wait to ask if I knew where Casa Blanca was in Riverside. I told him I used to live a mile and a half south of his old home. Shorty spun an elaborate story of his innocence in a double homicide. He said his lawyer told him he would get off, but when the verdict came back "Guilty," Shorty lost it and threw a glass water pitcher at the prosecuting attorney. Shorty said because of that incident, they now use only plastic water pitchers in Riverside Municipal courtrooms.

The next day Shorty brought in a photocopy of a newspaper clipping. The pitcher picture. I asked if he had committed other crimes that would have landed him in prison had he been caught. He admitted he had. I told him to pretend he was in prison for those crimes. He said the other crimes wouldn't have been for life. I considered telling him that had he been in prison for the other crimes, he couldn't have been charged with the double homicide. I didn't tell him.

At the open mike session on Sunday, I was astonished (I shouldn't have been, but I was) to see Crew get in line. The soft-spoken Muslim said he had now done a "360."

The pitchers are plastic in Vista too. I know because they want me.

The names were changed, but not to protect the innocent. None of us were.

DISCUSSION/REFLECTION QUESTIONS

CHAPTER 34   KAIROS 84

0. Imagine Cleat helping the reverend and Jerry pass out
    invitations to something Cleat himself desperately wanted to
    attend. Imagine a noisy gym packed with bunk beds and
    men.   Imagine seeing only one envelope left.   Do you think
    it would be too late to say one more prayer? Would you?

1. What is Jerry suggesting by saying: "The names were
    changed, but not to protect the innocent. None of us were"?

2. Do you see yourself as being as guilty as a man convicted of a
    double homicide? Would it make a difference on how you
    view and treat others if you saw yourself in the same dire
    straits as they are in? Explain.

3. Read Romans 3:10-18. Why is it important to fully grasp the
    depth of our guilt? Why is it important to realize how
    heinous even our smallest sin is to God? What difference
    would that realization make on how you relate to God? How
    would it affect your behavior?

4. Read Mark 15. What picture does this give of how God views
    your sin? What picture does it give of the value God places
    on your life? Is the same true for the prisoners in this story?
    The more we acknowledge our guilt, the more we appreciate
    God's love. The more we appreciate God's love, the more we
    love God. The more we acknowledge our guilt and appreciate
    God's love, the less we judge and the more we love. Pray a
    prayer confessing your sin and your guilt and expressing your
    love for Christ who was crucified to forgive that sin and
    remove that guilt.

CHAPTER 35   TECHNOLOGY

(Re: January 2011)

Dr. John Verkleeren said that although my aortic stenosis seemed to be getting worse and that I might need a heart valve replacement, it would be all right if we went on a week's vacation to nearby Coronado...as long as I took it easy. For the third year in a row, the weather for the second week in January on "The Island" was absolutely perfect and I was free of any anxiety.

On the third day there, my laptop (the same one that spent a month with me out in the field in Africa, the one that got dusty, dirty, beat up and scratched, but always functioned just fine) faded to black. We took it to an Apple store in San Diego. Happily for me, they quoted a low price, but said it would take a week, much longer than at any of their sister shops, because this was always an extremely busy store. We decided against going to another place of business, since we would be returning to the area in a week for my scheduled angiogram. I turned to leave, but then said, "Don't you need my name and number?" He waved something over my computer and said, "We already have your number, email, and home address, Mr. Maurer." Isn't modern technology great?

Before I tell what happened next, I must relate a few facts from before the turn of the century. Lorain, the wife of my carpool buddy Ed, does not use Novocaine or any other anesthetic when she visits the dentist! Now I am a paper-cut wimp who has always preferred the thick tongue, droopy lip, saggy cheek feeling to dental work sans some wonderful medicinal deadening agent. But when I asked my dentist, Dr. Richard (Rick) Goble, about Lorain's superhuman feat, he informed me that as one ages, the nerves tend to lose some of their sensitivity. Something from within forced me to say, "Can I try it?" (What was I thinking? This could be almost as bad as a paper cut.) Resolute, I put my resolve into action, and let him work on me without anesthetic!

Really! I didn't feel like a drooling largemouth bass afterward, either.

I know some of you are thinking, "Jerry, a paper cut? Honestly, man up!" But wait, when was the last time you had a real paper cut? You are working with some seemingly ordinary paper and suddenly, without warning, the knife-edge of a sole sheet slices the tip of one of your fingers. Not the back of the finger where there is much less sensitivity, but the absolute tip. Then later, when the throbbing has just ceased, you pick up something and the pulsing pain starts all over again. A minute after that, you pick up a piece of paper while your index finger points straight out, far from the offending page, because, unlike you, your index finger remembers what evil paper can do.

Another time I went to my medical provider for x-rays to see if I had kidney stones. When the technician pointed out that I certainly did, as evidenced by one kidney being clearly much larger than the other, she said I should be "crawling on the floor begging for medication." Yeah maybe, but had she ever seen someone with a paper cut?

And now, back to the story. While waiting in the hospital for a test, I noticed an apparent error in the paperwork they handed me. Some of the numbers in my "Vitals" read as follows: height 1.88 m and weight 95.255 kg. In the BMI (Body Mass Index) section, my Body Surface Area was noted as 2.23 square meters, but my BMI was listed as 26.95 kg/square meter. Well, I didn't need the calculator on my cell phone to figure out that 95 point low divided by 2 point lower would be nowhere near 26 point high. I imagined my anesthesiologist would be using my listed BMI to figure how much "stuff" to administer, and let me tell you, I wanted the right amount of "stuff." I figured I would point this out when I finally met the man whose hands would control my life.

Part of the check-in process includes a nurse asking some routine questions: Name? Birth date? Allergies? Smoker? Drinker? Religious preference? Followed by, "Is your will in order?" After noting my answers, she went to the bay on our right to ask a gentleman the same things. Only a thin cloth curtain and four yards of hospital air separated us. Adele and I heard him answer, "None" to religious preference and the apparent collective shock of husband and wife when asked, "Is your will in order?"

He and I lay in the hospital for the same reason: something in our respective chests wasn't working properly. Wouldn't it be fantastic if the problem could be fixed by having a simple angiogram turn into an angioplasty? Both procedures start with a teeny, tiny, shallow access slit in the crease where the leg meets the torso. The doctor then threads a small-diameter, guidable, flexible tube up through the femoral artery near and/or into the heart, where he checks certain areas (just checking = angiogram), and possibly enlarges a narrowed blood vessel with an expandable piece of tubing called a stent (stenting = angioplasty).

When the nurse left my curtained neighbor's bedside, the wife began telling horror stories she had heard or read of angiograms gone wrong. The atmospheres in the two bays were suddenly dynamic opposites. One was filled with a dark hopeless sense of doom knowing that the possible impending death would leave the wife alone and mark the absolute end of the existence of the husband.

The other bay held confidence.

The wife reminded her husband that they had agreed that if a stent were recommended, they would stop and talk it over with their doctor. When she said, "I hope you don't get a stent!" I considered going over and speaking with them. I could tell them what my two previous angiograms were like. I could tell them that if they found sizable blockages and did not stent them, the subsequent surgery would be dramatic--like going from a walk in the park to a swim under a polar ice cap. Both are doable with technology; one just takes a much longer recovery than the other.

I could tell them I believe we all have souls, and that what happens to each of our souls depends on a decision each one of us must make for ourselves...that no one else can decide for us. I could tell them I was at peace and without anxiety when death threatened, and that they could have that too. I could tell them that one of three things would likely happen to me in the operating room: they would install yet another stent near my heart; or they would perform yet another open-heart surgery, or I wouldn't live through it (statistically slight). I could tell them that that no matter what happened, I would be fine. I could tell them a lot, but I didn't.

A few hours later a nurse, Kim, asked me if I wanted some pills to make me feel relaxed. I told her I already was and thus skipped the medication. A little bit later she asked if I would like sedation and I revealed my astonishment with, "You mean I don't have to take sedation?" So I went in without it. (She was the "man" I was going to tell about the possible error in those "vitals'" numbers.) Dr. Rose painlessly deadened the area, made the small incision, and inserted the special tube. It felt like harmless bubbles being pumped in. That tube turned out to be too small, so he put in a larger tube, more bubbles. The technician, Wes, said it was more fun when the patient was awake (not drugged).

The blockage, as seen on the live monitor at the graft of my 1992 bypass to my right coronary artery, looked like a hotdog on a stick (a plump healthy artery abruptly becoming narrow). He said he was going to put in a stent. Good news! He indicated the length of the stent by showing me a small gap between his gloved thumb and index finger. For an instant I thought I should inform him he had some blood on his hands, and then I figured he already knew, and that the blood was mine.

Normally after an angiogram one gets clamped for about four hours to stop arterial bleeding at the incision and must lie motionless, flat on one's back. Wes said I would have to remain in that position for ten hours due to the use of the larger diameter tube. But because of several factors and my "awesome anatomy" he chose to use a Perclose, which meant I would have no clamps and must simply be cautious for a few hours. I told Wes to make certain he used his phrase "awesome anatomy" when he spoke with my wife.

Wes informed me that he and two others were going to move me off the operating table and that I should merely relax. I thought he got a team of three to help with the lifting. When I told him I weighed a tenth of a ton, he said it didn't matter. He then hit a switch that, slightly more than one second later, turned the deflated raft upon which I had been lying into a cocooned personal hovercraft. I literally floated on air to the adjacent gurney. The others stood by solely to make certain I didn't float too far! Momentum and lack of friction...you get the picture. The same thing happened when I got to my room. (I think it would be fun to have a few of those in a deserted gym, but that's just me.)

Once my room nurse confirmed my identity, she asked how I liked having no sedation. I asked how she knew. She said she read it in my chart, and that I was her first patient in two and a half years to have zero grams of sedation. So now I was feeling pretty special. Right before I checked out, I asked her to write that "no sedation" fact down and sign it—right there on the photocopy of one of my before-and-after fluoroscopic x-rays.

Two days later, minutes before a meeting at church, friends asked how it went. When I said I watched on the monitor, someone asked if I was awake, and I said I had declined sedation. I continued to think that my sedation-free status was sort of unique until Wayne Taylor, a technician who performs this procedure on a daily basis, said that most patients were awake. Funny, I don't remember if I told Adele what Wayne said.

Isn't it amazing what can be done with technology? Fixing a malady near a heart through a tiny opening in the leg! Fantastic! And speaking of technology, namely my computer, the Apple store tried to phone me to get clearance to start work because of an estimated few additional dollars. Unfortunately, they had called my abandoned landline number. (The only calls we used to get on it were from the governor, and then at two-year intervals.) They tried to email me, but they used my decade-old email address. So my computer sat there in its own hospital bay for a week, sick and broken, waiting for someone to rescue it. Yes, technology can be fantastic, but like the man in the bay to the right, if that is all you have, you don't have much.

DISCUSSION/REFLECTION QUESTIONS

CHAPTER 35 TECHNOLOGY

0. Moral dilemma: Jerry decided not to let the couple in the next bay know he had had two angiograms before and could possibly answer some of their questions. What would you have done? Why?

1. If you were facing a health issue that put your life at risk, how do you think you would respond? Rate yourself on a 1-10 scale with 1 being the inner peace Jerry was experiencing for his angiogram and 10 being the fear and gloom the couple next to him were experiencing.

2. Read Deuteronomy 31:8, Psalm 4:8, Psalm 23:4, Psalm 121, John 10:27-29 Hebrews 2:14-15. What do these Scriptures say can give us peace?

3. Read Romans 15:13 and Psalm 56:3-5. What do these verses say we must do in order to experience the peace God promise here?

4. How do we develop confidence in God's presence and power so that we can know peace in any situation? What steps do the following verses say we should take to develop the confidence that brings peace? Psalm 119:165, Psalm 23:1-3, Philippians 4:6-8, Psalm 95

EPILOGUE

CHAPTER 19   IRELAND

The French Prime Minister was Nicolas Sarkozy and in Rugby, the score was

Ireland 30, France 21.

I was the first to unpack. When I got to my little radio, I turned it on and, unbelievably, the voice had an Irish accent. I took it in to Adele so she could hear. We did not find out if the station was local, or eight times zones away.

Chapter 22   BOY MEETS GIRL

I asked Adele if this story was accurate and she said the number of command classes she was in seemed about right, but she might not have won one or two of them. (I called her mother, who said that she could not remember Adele ever breaking the streak.) Adele said the story was way too long and it looked like I was bragging. I said, "Check and check." I am blessed!

Chapter 24   BLINDED BY THE FACTS

Although Marilyn remembers swimming in the Grant's pool she does not remember me asking her that question. All I can say is it must have been one more silly unremarkable thing a five year old little brother says, but up until then it was the most shocking revelation I had ever heard.

Chapter 26   CHOICES

I do not remember what my fellow first graders said while Darrel Grapes was motionless; but I do remember how good it was to see him get up and say that he was okay.

"Choices" is the first of eleven major talks in a Kairos weekend. This was an adapted version a speech I gave in prison.

CHAPTER 29   CAT 2 (DOWN TO THE WIRE)

My brother Ralph remembers the cat in the box and the cat at the haystack as two different cats. He identified the "umbrella"

EPILOGUE Continued

tree as a carob tree. Also, he thinks the haystack incident took place in 1957 and not late 1956.

Furthermore, when my father, the cat, and I were looking at one another and the bucket, I opted to extend and exaggerate the scene for comic relief.

CHAPTER 30   Cat 3   (TOP OF THE TOWER)

While trying to determine the correct spelling of "Hananiah Zoe" I was pleasantly surprised to find a defunct website with his picture and the text of an interview he did with the Crystal Cathedral's Sheila Schuler Coleman. That interview told this same story and they spelled Hananiah's village "Sannaquellie." I was going to spell it "Sanakura" because that is what it sounded like when I heard Hananiah say it. While searching the spelling of Fofana, I found a Mohamed Fofana in Liberia. I do not know how many dozens or thousands of Mohamed Fofanas might live in Liberia. But this Mohamed Fofana was a professing Christian, and professing Christians in Liberia are rare indeed. Also, this Mohamed Fofana was in Monrovia! Here is a portion of the article:

"On Sunday 10 February 2002, 39 young men and boys were reportedly rounded up from various churches around Monrovia and forcibly taken to a field near Duala market...

"On 15 February, a fleeing woman, MS, witnessed nine men being seized in Clara Town, Bushrod Island, and was later told that they were taken to the 'front line' by Liberian security forces. The woman knew three of the nine men who were seized. They were Mohamed Fofana, Thomas Dukuly, and Jerry Weefor. Their relatives reported being concerned for their safety as they have not heard from them since. (Sadly, I, Jerry Maurer, believe this to mean fellow Christian, Mohamed Fofana, is probably dead.)

"On 19 February in Tubmanburg, Bomi County, four men were reportedly tortured by members of the ATU under suspicion of being "dissidents." One man died as a result of the torture and was seen lying near the other three men. (Note: The squeamish should stop reading at this point.) According to a witness who spoke to the three men, one of the men denied he was a dissident and described how his scrotum had been hammered flat by a member of the ATU. The two other men were too fearful to say anything but, according to the witness, they were clearly in pain. A member of the ATU, who was nearby, warned that this information should not be made public."

Chapter 31   DIXIE

The song referred to in the story is a reworded version of "In the Jungle" by Ron Perry. (In the city in Davis's city, the Lion sleeps tonight.)

Mike Umbenhaur, my brother-in-law, was visiting in a coffee shop he frequents called "Jitters." Pictures line the walls; Mike was looking at a new one of the Luxor, but with the light out of kilter. Soon, a man of about seventy years came up and informed Mike that he was the photographer of the picture. Mike said he liked the image because it showed imperfection. The two talked and soon discovered they had each come to live in Las Vegas for similar reasons after becoming widowers. As Mike got up to leave, he realized he hadn't introduced himself. After hearing his name the man asked if they knew each other.

Mike said, "No, I would remember."

The elderly independent photographer asked, "What is your name again?" Upon hearing it, the man continued, "Yes, about a year ago I was visiting in Philadelphia and the Sunday sermon was about a woman named Umbenhaur in California who died of cancer." An astonished Mike informed him that the woman was his wife, Dixie. The response was, "Yes, that was her name, Dixie."

Mike stood there and simply cried. The cameraman asked if he had upset him. Mike answered, "No, quite the opposite."

A Prayer for Salvation

Dear Jesus,

I am a sinner. I have disobeyed you and broken your commandments. I am wrong and need your forgiveness and new life. I believe you are the Son of God. I believe you died on the cross to forgive my sin. I believe you rose from the dead and have the power to give me new life. I now surrender my life to you and ask you to come into my life and take over. I am choosing to be your follower. Thank you for your forgiveness. Thank you for coming into my life. Now walk with me and give me the power to turn from doing wrong and start doing what is right. Amen!

To order more copies of
"From Jer to Eternity"

Go to:

Lulu.com, in the search box near the top select "Books" then type in "From Jer to Eternity"

OR

For about a buck more (which Amazon will keep) go to:

Amazon.com, type in "From Jer to Eternity"

OR

If you are having a problem contact our sales manager at The Farmer and Adele Publishing:

JerryRMaurer@gmail.com   (Notice the fifth "R".)

All profits from sales of this book, beyond printing and shipping costs, will go to faithalive365.com and the African orphan project sponsored by the independent church at 463 S. Stagecoach in Fallbrook, CA, 92028.

To contact the Chief Editor please reach him at:

JerryRMaurer@gmail.com

To contact the author use:

JerryRMaurer@gmail.com

To register a complaint please contact Mia in Customer Satisfaction:

MiaCulpa@bleedingheart.org